SCIENTIFIC CHINESE COMMUNICATION：
MATERIALS SCIENCE

科技汉语口语交流

材料科学卷

翟华嶂　邢清清　陈　慧　著

版权专有　侵权必究

图书在版编目（CIP）数据

科技汉语口语交流. 材料科学卷 / 翟华嶂，邢清清，陈慧著. --北京：北京理工大学出版社，2022.1
  ISBN 978 - 7 - 5763 - 0865 - 5

Ⅰ. ①科… Ⅱ. ①翟… ②邢… ③陈… Ⅲ. ①材料科学—汉语—口语—对外汉语教学—教材 Ⅳ. ①H195.4

中国版本图书馆 CIP 数据核字（2022）第 014899 号

出版发行 / 北京理工大学出版社有限责任公司
社　　址 / 北京市海淀区中关村南大街 5 号
邮　　编 / 100081
电　　话 / （010）68914775（总编室）
　　　　　　（010）82562903（教材售后服务热线）
　　　　　　（010）68944723（其他图书服务热线）
网　　址 / http://www.bitpress.com.cn
经　　销 / 全国各地新华书店
印　　刷 / 保定市中画美凯印刷有限公司
开　　本 / 787 毫米 × 1092 毫米　1/16
印　　张 / 13.25　　　　　　　　　　　　　　　责任编辑 / 徐　宁
字　　数 / 192 千字　　　　　　　　　　　　　　文案编辑 / 把明宇
版　　次 / 2022 年 1 月第 1 版　2022 年 1 月第 1 次印刷　　责任校对 / 周瑞红
定　　价 / 58.00 元　　　　　　　　　　　　　　责任印制 / 李志强

图书出现印装质量问题，请拨打售后服务热线，本社负责调换

前　　言

留学生科技汉语沟通能力培养是汉语国际教育未来再上新台阶的必经之路。中国已经成为亚洲最大的留学目的国，但研究生比例仍然偏低。以2018年为例，在华近50万留学生中，有52%的学生攻读学位，其中研究生约占整体比例的17%，理工科学生比例占32%。国家政策也对留学生使用汉语进行沟通的能力提出了要求。根据《来华留学生高等教育质量规范（试行）》，"以中文为专业教学语言的学科、专业中，来华留学生应当能够顺利使用中文完成本学科、专业的学习和研究任务，并具备使用中文从事本专业相关工作的能力；毕业时中文能力应当达到《国际汉语能力标准》五级水平"。如何提升在中国留学的理工科研究生的科技汉语沟通能力，是汉语国际教育的努力方向之一。

《科技汉语口语交流：材料科学卷》立足于"交际教学法"的语言学习理念，以尼日利亚学生 B. Emmanuel 来到中国留学，在北京理工大学材料学院攻读博士学位的过程为线索，通过展示校园生活和科研经历中的口语对话场景，培养学习者自学运用科技汉语进行口头交际的能力。

本书的目标读者是已经具备初、中级汉语基础并拥有一定理工专业基础知识的汉语学习者。通过口语对话引入材料科学的学科知识和前沿研究的概念、术语以及惯用科技汉语表达，引导读者熟悉校园学习生活场景，体验科研工作的不同阶段，从而通过使用汉语，更自如地融入中国研究型大学的科研环境。

本书是融合了互联网技术的新形态语言教材。通过再现留学生在校园生活学习的真实场景，模拟学习者日常生活和专业学习对话。学习者可以扫描各个章节中的二维码来观看与课程情节相关联的短视频，从而利用视觉和听觉感官，增强语言学习的效果。本书编写采用中文、拼音、英文对照模式，并在每小节课后给出重点词汇，便于学习者根据个人兴趣和工作需要自主选择学习内容。

本书由北京理工大学国际交流合作处牵头编写，编者分别来自北京理工大学材料学院、外国语学院和留学生中心。撰写过程得到了材料学院多个课题组的有力支持。拉各斯大学孔子学院的前任中方院长姜丽蓉教授、王永静教授、现任中方院长赵宏凌教授作为专家组成员审阅了初稿。课程短视频的脚本由北京理工大学法学院张爱秀博士编写。视频拍摄工作得到了学校宣传部王征副部长的大力支持，国际交流合作处毛宇峰副处长统筹协调，苗旻、李一博、吴迪、彭姝等多位同志参与拍摄，由宣传部郭广泽等同志完成拍摄和后期剪辑。

目 录

第一章 留学北理 共筑一梦
dì yī zhāng　liú xué běi lǐ　gòng zhù yī mèng

Studying in BIT to Realize Your Dream ·············· 1

1.1 入学指南 Getting Started ·············· 1
rù xué zhǐ nán

1.1.1 留学中国 Studying in China ·············· 1
liú xué zhōng guó

1.1.2 北理一瞥 Facts About Beijing Institute of Technology ·············· 6
běi lǐ yī piē

1.1.3 申请流程 Applying for Admission ·············· 13
shēn qǐng liú chéng

1.1.4 收到通知 Receiving the Offer ·············· 18
shōu dào tōng zhī

1.2 北京理工大学校园生活
běi jīng lǐ gōng dà xué xiào yuán shēng huó

Living and Studying in BIT ·············· 21

1.2.1 食在北理 Eating at the Cafeteria ·············· 21
shí zài běi lǐ

1.2.2 点菜用餐 Ordering Food ·············· 26
diǎn cài yòng cān

1.2.3 北理工足球 BIT Soccer Team ·············· 29
běi lǐ gōng zú qiú

1.2.4 学在图书馆 Studying in the Library ·············· 34
xué zài tú shū guǎn

1.2.5 便捷的快递 Convenient Express Delivery Service ·············· 44
biàn jié de kuài dì

· 1 ·

1.2.6 交往礼节 Social Etiquette ·········· 50

1.2.7 北理工国际文化节 BIT International Culture Festival ·········· 53

第二章 材以养德，料以治学
Studying Fine Materials for Knowledge and Virtue ·········· 59

2.1 材料学院概述 Overview of the School of MSE ·········· 59

2.2 参观材料学院 Visiting the School of MSE ·········· 73

2.3 材料科学的研究课题 Research Topics in the School of MSE
·········· 91

2.3.1 功能有机高分子Ⅰ——聚集诱导发光材料
Functional Polymer Ⅰ—Aggregation Induced Emission ·········· 91

2.3.2 功能有机高分子Ⅱ——阻燃材料
Functional Polymer Ⅱ—Flame Retardant Materials ·········· 98

2.3.3 功能有机高分子Ⅲ——生物医用材料
Functional Polymer Ⅲ—Biomedical Materials ·········· 103

2.3.4 功能有机高分子Ⅳ——天然高分子材料
Functional Polymer Ⅳ—Natural Polymer Materials ·········· 109

2.3.5 电子封装技术 Electronic Packaging Technology ·········· 112

2.3.6 新能源材料与器件 New Energy Materials and Devices ·········· 120

2.3.7 低维功能纳米材料
Low-dimensional Functional Nanomaterials ·········· 128

第三章 学有所成 不负韶华
Succeed in Research, Paying off the Youth ······ 139

3.1 材料实验室生存法则
Survive at Materials Laboratory ······ 139

3.2 实验室的工作和生活 Work and Life at Laboratory ······ 147

3.3 课题组的组会 Group Seminar ······ 169

3.4 材料样品的表征与测试
Characterization and Testing of Material Samples ······ 177

3.5 撰写科学论文 Writing a Scientific Manuscript ······ 184

3.6 准备学位答辩的流程
Procedures for the Defense of the Academic Degree ······ 191

跋 ······ 200

第一章 留学北理 共筑一梦
Studying in BIT to Realize Your Dream

导引

1.1 入学指南
Getting Started

1.1.1 留学中国
Studying in China

中国大学概况

Emmanuel Bolarinwa 是尼日利亚地方大学的一名青年物理教师。3月,他的朋友 Khalid 刚从中国留学归来,Emmanuel 去拜访他,并想了解在中国留学的情况。

Emmanuel Bolarinwa is a young physics teacher in a Nigeria local college. Khalid, Emmanuel's friend, just returned from studying in China in March. Emmanuel is visiting him to get some information about studying in China.

Emmanuel：嗨,Khalid！听说你去中国留学了,现在已经毕业了吗？

Hi, Khalid! I heard you were studying in China. Have you graduated yet?

Khalid: 嗨，Emmanuel！好久不见！我刚拿到了我的博士学位，前天才从中国回来。

Hi, Emmanuel! Long time no see! I just received my Ph. D. degree there and came back from China the day before yesterday.

Emmanuel: 恭喜你，Khalid 博士！你感觉在中国的学习和生活怎么样？

Congratulations, Dr. Khalid! How do you feel about your study and life in China?

Khalid: 很好！去中国留学对我来说是一个非常正确的选择，也是一段非常棒的体验！

Fantastic experience! It has been one of my best choices to study in China, and it was a great experience!

Emmanuel: 最近我正在考虑出国深造，但是还没有确定要去哪个国家，你可以帮我参考一下吗？

I've been thinking about furthering my studies abroad lately, but I haven't decided which country yet. Can you help me in this regard?

Khalid: 那我肯定推荐去中国啦。中国有着繁荣的经济，多元的文化，先进的科学技术。尤其是，还有热情友好的中国人，是出国留学的最佳选择之一。

I recommend China! China is well-known for its prosperous economy, diverse culture and advanced science and technology. Chinese people are very friendly and welcoming. Studying in China is one of the best choices for studying abroad.

Emmanuel：听起来不错。那么，中国的大学多吗？

Sounds good. How many universities are there in China?

Khalid：中国已经成为整个亚洲拥有顶尖大学最多的国家。前不久我刚看到一个数据报告：截至2018年3月30日，中国教育部宣布全国性的高等院校共有2 688所，其中本科院校1 265所，不乏有在全世界范围内都享有盛誉、实力极强的大学。

China already has more top universities than any other country in Asia. I just read a report several days before: On March 30, 2018, the Ministry of Education of China announced that there are 2,688 institutions of higher education in China, with 1,265 issuing Bachelor's Degree. Some of them are world renowned universities with research strength.

Emmanuel：那可真不少！我打算学习工程类专业，然后成为一名工程师的话，应该怎样选择呢？

That is a big number! My intention is to be an engineer after graduation so I will probably need to study engineering. Then how should I choose?

Khalid：在中国高校圈里有一个"卓越大学联盟"*，又称为E9联盟，这个联盟九所大学的工程类专业都是一流的。

There is an "Alliance of Excellence" in China known as the *E9 Universities*, with 9 universities being the first-rate in engineering education.

Emmanuel：厉害！那我要认真考虑一下去中国留学，希望有机会留在中国当工程师。

Great! In that case I will get down to consider studying in China and then staying in China as an engineer.

Khalid：如果想要在中国做一名工程师，首先你必须掌握一门专业的知识和技能，比如：材料学、电子学、机械工程等。其次，你还要学习中文，了解中国文化。

To be an engineer in China, you must first learn to get relevant knowledge and skills in a specific field, such as materials science, electronics, mechanical engineering, etc. Besides, you must learn Chinese and understand Chinese culture.

Emmanuel：我对中国文化也很感兴趣，但是学习中文会不会很难？

I am interested in Chinese culture as well. Is it difficult to learn Chinese language?

Khalid：中文学习并不难。只要拥有浓厚的兴趣、强烈的动机加上认真努力的付出，相信你一定可以学得好，用得好。

Not as hard as it sounds like. As long as there is a keen interest and strong motivation coupled with serious efforts, you will learn it well and use it skillfully.

Emmanuel：
hǎo de　xiè xiè nǐ　wǒ huì hǎo hǎo kǎo lǜ
好的，谢谢你。我会好好考虑。
OK, thanks, I will think it over.

Khalid：
bù kè qì
不客气。
No problem.

重点词汇
Keywords & expressions

尼日利亚	Nigeria
物理	physics
博士学位	Ph. D. degree
出国留学	study abroad
文化	culture
工程师	engineer
卓越大学联盟	Alliance of Excellence, Excellence 9, E9
材料学	materials science
电子学	electronics
机械工程	mechanic engineering

*"卓越大学联盟"（Excellence 9, E9），全称是"卓越人才培养合作高校联盟"。2010年11月，由北京理工大学、哈尔滨工业大学、同济大学、东南大学、天津大学、

西北工业大学、华南理工大学、大连理工大学和重庆大学等九所具有理工特色的重点综合性大学本着"追求卓越、协同创新"的原则,共同签署《卓越人才培养合作框架协议》,开展教育、科研、国际合作等领域的全方位合作。

1.1.2 北理一瞥
Facts About Beijing Institute of Technology

北京理工大学概况

几天后,Emmanuel 和 Khalid 又见面了。Emmanuel 下定决心要申请去中国留学,但是不知道应该选择去哪一所大学,Khalid 向 Emmanuel 推荐了自己留学所在的学校——北京理工大学。

A few days later, Emmanuel and Khalid meet again. Emmanuel has decided to apply for studying in China. However he still hasn't decided which university to choose. Khalid recommends his Alma Mater-Beijing Institute of Technology.

Khalid: Emmanuel,上次你说想去中国留学,考虑得怎么样?

Emmanuel, you said you were thinking of studying in China, any news?

第一章 留学北理共筑一梦

Emmanuel：我在网上查了一下，确实中国有很多不错的大学，但我现在不知道该怎么选择。你可以给我一些建议吗？

I checked some information online, there are many good universities in China indeed, but it's really hard for me to make a decision on which one to choose. Could you give me some advice?

Khalid：你希望去哪个城市，想要读什么专业呢？

Which city would you like to go, and which major do you want to apply?

Emmanuel：我想去中国的首都，北京，希望去那里读工程类的专业。

I would like to study at the engineering program in the capital city of China, Beijing.

Khalid：不错，那我推荐你去我的母校——北京理工大学，你也可以简称为北理工。

Good choice, then I recommend you my Alma Mater—Beijing Institute of Technology. You may also call it BIT for short.

BIT 简笔画

BIT Stick Figure

Emmanuel：太好了，你能给我介绍一下北京理工大学吗？

Great! Could you give me a brief introduction on Beijing Institute of Technology?

Khalid：当然可以！北京理工大学创立于1940年，它是首批进入中国高校建设的"211工程"和"985工程"，首批进入"世界一流大学"建设高校A类行列的中国重点大学。

Sure! Founded in 1940, Beijing Institute of Technology has always been a key member university selected in the state elite university developing programs – 985 Project and 211 project and also in the national "Double First-Class" program aiming to promote the development of world-class universities and disciplines in China.

Emmanuel：我听说，在中国如果一所大学属于"211工程"、"985工程"或者"世界一流大学建设高校"，就说明这所大学非常厉害。

I have heard that if a university in China is selected in "211 project", "985 project" or "Double First-Class" project, it means that this university is highly reputed.

Khalid：那当然了，在英国QS教育集团发布的2022世界大学排行榜中，北理工位居世界第392名、亚洲第76名、中国大陆第18名呢！

That's correct! According to UK QS World University Rankings 2022, BIT ranks 392nd among the "Top 500 universities," 76th in Asia, and 18th in Mainland, China.

Emmanuel： 太酷了！那么北理工是以什么专业为主呢？

Cool! What programs does BIT offer?

Khalid： 北理工的专业是以理工科为主，工、理、管、文协调发展的，而且多数专业排名进入了中国高校的前十名。

BIT in its tradition has been focusing on the advancement of science and technology but has also developed other areas, such as management and humanities, with numerous majors ranking top 10 among Chinese universities.

Emmanuel： 听起来很强哎！今后我想成为一名工程师的话，北理工可太适合我了。

Sounds nice! I dream to be an engineer, and I think BIT will be perfect for me.

Khalid： 对呀，你不是想当一名材料科学工程师吗？北理工的材料科学与工程学科实力强劲，培养了许多优秀的工程师。

Right, don't you wish to be an engineer in Materials Science? This program is well recognized in BIT, and most of its graduates have become excellent engineers.

Emmanuel： 北理工的师资力量怎么样，在校学生有多少？

How many faculties and students are there in BIT?

Khalid： 北理工的师资力量雄厚，一线专职教师有2 200余人，全日制在校生达到2.8万余人。

There are more than 2,200 front-line full-time faculties and more than 28,000 full-time students.

Emmanuel：哇，看来北理工专业齐备，规模也很大，在中国的知名度也很高。那它是一所国际化的大学吗？它和其他国家的高校有合作项目吗？

Wow! Thanks for the introduction, I think BIT has complete programs and is quite comprehensive, as well as being very famous in China. What about its international reputation? Does it cooperate with universities from other countries?

Khalid：百分之百是！北理工已经与六大洲71个国家和地区的270多所高校签订校级合作协议，与德国慕尼黑工业大学、亚琛工业大学、俄罗斯莫斯科罗蒙诺索夫大学、日本东京工业大学、加拿大北阿尔伯塔理工学院、美国伊利诺伊理工大学等50多所国际知名院校设立学生交换项目，形成了人才培养国际化的全球网络。

Absolutely! BIT has established collaborative ties with more than 350 universities of 75 countries and regions on six continents. To establish a global network of talent cultivation, it has set up student exchange programs with more than 50 partner universities, such as The Technical University of Munich (TUM), RWTH Aachen University, University of Moskoromonosov, Tokyo Institute of Technology, Northern Alberta Institute of Technology, and Illinois Institute of Technology.

Emmanuel：那么在北理工学习的外国留学生多吗？

Are there many international students studying in BIT?

Khalid：非常多！北理工的国际化水平和国际影响力在不断提升，"留学北理"已形成品牌，每年都会有很多学生申请。例如，2019年就有来自149个国家的2 500多名外国留学生在校学习和生活，而且超过70%的留学生来自"一带一路"沿线的国家和地区。

Yes！BIT is gaining more influence in the world and is now regarded as one of the best destinations for international students studying in China. Studying in BIT has become a new trend. For example, in 2019, BIT was home to 2,500 international students from 149 different countries, 70% of whom come from the countries in the "Belt and Road Initiative."

留学北理
Studying in BIT

Emmanuel：真棒！那我要申请北京理工大学的材料科学与
工程专业，攻读博士学位。
Terrific! I will apply for the Ph. D. program of Materials Science and Engineering at Beijing Institute of Technology.

Khalid：太好了，你也做出了一个很正确的选择。如果
有需要的话，我会给你发一些申请相关的信息。
Fantastic. You have also made a wise choice. I will send you the necessary information about application.

Emmanuel：太感谢了！
Thanks a million!

Khalid：别客气。祝你成功！
You are welcome. Wish you success!

重点词汇

Keywords & expressions

北京理工大学	Beijing Institute of Technology，BIT
专业	major
985 工程	985 Project
学科	discipline
材料科学与工程	Materials Science and Engineering，MSE
留学北理	study in BIT
一带一路	Belt and Road Initiative

1.1.3 申请流程 Applying for Admission

申请奖学金

Emmanuel 在申请的过程中遇到了一些问题，于是他电话联系了负责招生的陈老师。

Emmanuel encountered some problems in the application process, so he called Ms. Chen, who is in charge of admissions at BIT.

陈：喂，你好！这里是北京理工大学留学生中心。请问有什么需要帮助的？

Hello! Office of International Students, Beijing Institute of Technology. How can I help you?

Emmanuel：喂，陈老师，你好！我是来自尼日利亚的 Emmanuel Bolarinwa，我想申请你们学校的博士研究生。

Hello, Ms. Chen! I am Emmanuel from Nigeria. I would like to apply for your Ph. D. program.

陈：好的，欢迎你申请北京理工大学！你对什么专业感兴趣？

Thank you for your interest in Beijing Institute of Technology. What is your question?

Emmanuel：谢谢陈老师。我想攻读材料科学与工程专业的博士学位，请问你们学校提供奖学金吗？

Thanks, I want to apply for the Ph. D. program of materials science and engineering. May I know about the scholarship offered by your university?

陈: 我们学校有非常完善的奖学金体系。对于硕士和博士项目，你可以申请中国政府奖学金。

We have very complete and strong scholarship programs. You may apply for the Chinese Government Scholarships for master and Ph. D. programs.

Emmanuel: 我听说过。我身边好些同学和朋友都是通过申请这个奖学金来中国留学的。你能简单介绍一下吗？

I see. Some of my classmates and friends went to study in China under the Chinese Government Scholarships.

陈: 中国政府奖学金是由中国政府设立的，用以鼓励培养知华友华的外国友人来华学习。全额的中国政府奖学金包含学费、住宿费、综合医疗保险费和生活费。

The Chinese Government Scholarships is set up by the Chinese government to encourage foreign applicants to come and study in China. Full Chinese Government Scholarships covers tuition, accommodation, comprehensive medical insurance and living subsidy.

Emmanuel: 真是太慷慨了！那请问研究生的学制是几年？

That's very generous! What is the duration of learning of the graduate

第一章 留学北理共筑一梦

programs?

陈：通常情况，博士学制是4年，硕士学制是2年。
Generally speaking, four years for Ph. D. programs, and two years for master programs.

Emmanuel：我有点担心我的中文不够好，我可以用英文学习吗？
I don't speak much Chinese. Can I study in English?

陈：可以的，北理工所有的博士专业都是全英文指导，材料科学与工程专业也是。不过申请英文专业需要有英语语言水平的证明。
Sure, all Ph. D. programs are conducted in English, as well as the program of materials science and engineering. English proficiency certificate is required for English programs.

Emmanuel：我的雅思成绩是7.0分，应该满足这个条件。不过，如果我选择了英文项目，我还能学习中文吗？我真的很想学习中文。
My IELTS score is 7.0, which should be Okay. However, if I choose the English program, do I still have the chance to learn Chinese? I really want to learn it.

陈：可以。为了帮助留学生了解中国，了解中国文化，快速融入中国的生活，我们为所有留学生开设了中文语言课和中国概况课。
Yes. In order to help international students understand China and

Chinese culture, we have offered Chinese lessons and Glimpse of China for all our students.

Emmanuel：那太好了！对了，我自硕士毕业后在大学里当物理教师，这个会有优势吗？

That would be great! I've been working as a physics teacher since I got my master degree. Is it helpful to my application?

陈：这是你申请的优势，因为青年教师是我们优先招收的生源，目前有近30%的在校留学生都是各国高校的优秀青年教师。

This is an advantage for your application, as junior faculties from the universities are welcome in our admission. At present, nearly 30% of the international students in BIT are junior faculty members from their home universities.

Emmanuel：真的吗？那我太开心了。我从网上了解了需要提交的申请材料，我不太明白其中的一个材料。请问北理工导师的推荐信是什么？

Really? Happy to know that. I have learned about the required application materials, but I don't quite understand the BIT supervisor's recommendation letter. What is it?

陈：这里是说你需要联系材料科学与工程专业的研究生导师，并且获得他的推荐信。导师会通过邮件、电话或者学术视频面试来了解你。如果他认为你具有培养潜质，而且你的学习背景、研究兴趣和他的研究领域一致，那么导师就会给你出具推荐信了。

It means that you need to contact a supervisor of materials science and engineering and get his academic recommendation. The supervisor will communicate with you by email, telephone or video interview. If he or she thinks you have the academic potentials, and your background, research interests are in line with his or her research field, you will get a recommendation letter.

Emmanuel：听起来有点儿挑战性，但是我会尽力好好准备材料的。

Sounds rather challenging, but I will try my best to prepare the documents.

陈：祝你好运！如果你还需要任何帮助，请随时与我们联系。

Good luck to you! Please let us know if you need any help.

Emmanuel：非常感谢，陈老师再见！

Thank you so much. Goodbye, Ms. Chen.

陈：感谢来电，再见，Emmanuel！

Thanks for calling. Bye bye, Emmanuel.

北京理工大学 + 校徽

Beijing Institute of Technology + the School Badge

zhòng diǎn cí huì
重 点 词 汇
Keywords & expressions

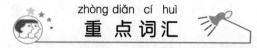

申请	apply for
留学生中心	Office of International Students
中国政府奖学金	Chinese Government Scholarships
学费	tuition
综合医疗保险费	comprehensive medical insurance
学制	duration of learning
雅思	IELTS（International English Language Testing System）
导师	supervisor
推荐信	recommendation letter
视频面试	video interview

1.1.4 收到通知
Receiving the Offer

　　jīng guò jǐ gè yuè bù duàn de lián xì hé shēn qǐng　　　　　　zhōng yú shōu dào
　　经 过 几 个 月 不 断 的 联 系 和 申 请，Emmanuel 终 于 收 到
le lái zì běi jīng lǐ gōng dà xué de lù qǔ tōng zhī shū　　tā fēi cháng gāo xìng　　lì kè
了 来 自 北 京 理 工 大 学 的 录 取 通 知 书。他 非 常 高 兴，立 刻
gěi　　　　dǎ diàn huà fēn xiǎng zhè ge xǐ xùn
给 Khalid 打 电 话 分 享 这 个 喜 讯。

　　After months of constant contact and application, Emmanuel finally received the admission notice from Beijing Institute of Technology. He is in seventh heaven, and calls Khalid at the first time to share the good news.

　　　　　　　　　　wèi　　　　　　　gào sù nǐ yī gè hǎo xiāo xi　　wǒ bèi běi jīng lǐ gōng dà
Emmanuel：喂，Khalid，告 诉 你 一 个 好 消 息，我 被 北 京 理 工 大

第一章　留学北理共筑一梦

学录取啦！

Hello, Khalid, a good news, I have been admitted to Beijing Institute of Technology!

Khalid: 真的吗?! 恭喜你成为我的学弟！我们都是北理工的学生了。

Really?! Congratulations to my old boy! We are both BITers now.

Emmanuel: 我还得到了中国政府奖学金的资助呢, 太开心了, 非常感谢你给我的建议和帮助！

I feel so blessed to be offered the Chinese Government Scholarships and I really appreciate your advice and help.

Khalid: 哇, 那真是值得庆祝, 我为你感到高兴！接下来你按照他们的要求准备留学相关的物件和资料就可以了。

Wow, that's really something to celebrate! I am so happy for you! Next just get ready for what you need when they ask you to prepare.

Emmanuel: 好的, 刚才我收到了一个快递, 里面有录取通知书、签证申请表和入学须知。须知上面详细解释了报到注册相关的各种事项, 例如应怎么准备什么、怎么到达学校等。

Sure, I just received an EMS package with an admission notice, a visa application form, a notice of instructions on registration and orientation preparation, explaining all details. Such as how to prepare the trip, how to reach BIT, etc.

Khalid：真贴心！学校要求什么时候报到？

That's very considerate! When should you register?

Emmanuel：9月2日-3日。

September 2nd and 3rd.

Khalid：好，那你赶快申请签证吧。我想你还可以开始学习一点中文，非常有用的。有什么问题再联系我。

OK, then apply for the visa as soon as possible. I think you may start to learn some Chinese, which is quite helpful. Let me know if there is any problem.

Emmanuel：好的，谢谢你为我做的一切！

Sure, thanks for everything!

我们都爱北理工
We all love BIT

重点词汇
Keywords & expressions

录取通知书	admission notice
签证	visa
注册	registration

1.2 北京理工大学校园生活
Living and Studying in BIT

1.2.1 食在北理
Eating at the Cafeteria

校园卡充值　　　在食堂就餐

Emmanuel 刚刚来到北京理工大学，周围的一切对他都是新鲜而又陌生的。他想去吃午饭，但不知道食堂在哪里。于是，他向路过的中国学生求助。

Emmanuel has just arrived at Beijing Institute of Technology, and everything around him was new and strange. He wants to have lunch, but he doesn't know where to go. Then, he asks a Chinese student on his way for help.

Emmanuel：嗨，同学！请问您是本学校的学生吗？

Hi, excuse me, are you from BIT?

赵: 你好！是的，我是本校的学生。我叫赵阳，你是新生吧？

Hi! Yes, I'm studying here. I am Zhao Yang. You are new here, right?

Emmanuel: 对，我是昨天刚刚入学的，请叫我Emmanuel。我想去吃午饭，可是不知道该去哪儿。

Yes, I just arrived yesterday. Please call me Emmanuel. I want to have lunch, but I don't know where to go.

赵: 校园里有很多食堂和餐厅，你想吃什么样的饭菜？

There are lots of dining halls and canteens on campus. What would you like to eat?

Emmanuel: 我想尝试一下中国菜，听说中国菜特别好吃。

I want to try Chinese food. I heard it's very delicious.

赵: 北京理工大学食堂的饭菜非常可口，好吃不贵。"清华的牌子，北理的饭"已经成为流传很广的名句。校园里有七个食堂，食堂里的菜种类繁多，你可以品尝到各式有名的中国菜肴，比如宫保鸡丁、麻婆豆腐、鱼香肉丝等；也有西式快餐，比如三明治、汉堡、薯条等。还有大大小小的店面，比如饺子馆、重庆小面、百万庄园等，散布在校园内的各个角落，几乎是想吃什么就能有什么。

The meal in the BIT's canteen is very delicious, and not expensive. Dinner at BIT enjoys a reputation of "Tsinghua Quality"! There are seven dining halls and canteens in total on campus, which offer a variety of Chinese cuisines, like Kung Pao Chicken, Mapo Tofu, Shredded Pork with Garlic Sauce, etc. You may also find western fast food, like hamburgers, sandwiches, French fries and so on. There are stores of all sizes, such as Dumplings House, Chongqing Street Noodles and Byone Restaurant, scattered around the campus. You can find almost anything you would like to have.

Emmanuel：听起来真不错，我感觉更饿了。

Sounds great! I feel hungrier now.

赵：如果是朋友聚会，还可以去理工餐厅，延园餐馆或者金榜缘餐馆。在这些餐馆可以点菜，环境也很不错。

There are canteens for friends gathering, such as Ligong Canteen, Yanyuan Restaurant, or Jinbangyuan Restaurant, where you can order food and enjoy good dining environment.

Emmanuel：那太好了。

That's great!

赵：你喜欢吃辣的吗？中国最有名的菜系之一是川菜，非常辣，却很有味道。

Do you like spicy food? One of the most famous cuisines in China is Sichuan cuisine, which is very spicy but tastes so good.

Emmanuel：不好意思，我不能吃太辣的。

Sorry that I don't eat much spicy food.

赵：啊，那就去7号食堂吧，品尝一下有名的北京烤鸭套餐，特制的鸭肉蘸上甜面酱，就着黄瓜条，裹在荷叶饼里，是地道的北京风味。

Ah, let's go to No. 7 Dining Hall to try the famous Beijing Roast Duck, which is special roasted duck meat dipped in sweet soybean paste with cucumber sticks and wrapped in a thin pancake. It's authentic Beijing style.

Emmanuel：改天我一定要去尝一尝。

I must try it sometime.

赵：对了，我们还有清真食堂，可以提供多种多样的清真食物，很多留学生都喜欢去那里吃饭。

By the way, there is a halal dining hall providing a great variety of halal meals. Many international students prefer to go there.

Emmanuel：请问我可以和你一起去吃饭吗？想请你推荐几款好吃的饭菜。

May I go with you? Please recommend some delicious dishes to me.

赵：没问题，正好我也要去吃午饭。

No problem, I am on the way to lunch.

Emmanuel：在食堂里怎么付钱？

Well, by the way, how do I pay there?

赵：我们用校园卡支付。如果你的卡里没有钱，可以先用手机充值。

Usually we pay with the campus card. If there is no money in your card, you may top it up with your smart phone first.

Emmanuel：什么?！用手机充值校园卡？

What?! Top up the card with a phone?

赵：对，我平时出门都不用带钱包和现金，带上手机就可以了。已经是信息化时代了，在北京买东西、坐公交利用手机支付方便又快捷，很快你就知道了。现在我先教你给校园卡充值吧。

Yes, I don't need to take my wallet or cash when I go out with my mobile phone. It's convenient and fast to pay by mobile phone in Beijing. You'll find it out soon. Now let me recharge the campus card for you.

Emmanuel：哇，这么方便，真是大开眼界！

Wow, so convenient. What an eye-opening day!

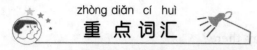 重点词汇
Keywords & expressions

食堂	dining hall/cafeteria
餐厅	canteen
宫保鸡丁	Kung Pao Chicken
豆腐	tofu
餐馆	restaurant
辣的	spicy
菜系	cuisine
北京烤鸭	Beijing Roast Duck
清真餐厅	halal dining hall

1.2.2 点菜用餐
Ordering Food

Emmanuel 和赵阳来到了清真食堂，Emmanuel 还是不知道该吃些什么。

Emmanuel and Zhao Yang come to the halal dining hall, but Emmanuel still doesn't know what to eat.

赵：Emmanuel，这儿有各式饭菜，你想吃什么？
Emmanuel, all kinds of dishes here, what do you what to eat?

Emmanuel：我想吃富富和苏亚。
I want to eat fufuo and suya.

第一章 留学北理共筑一梦

赵：什么是富富和苏亚？我们这儿没有。

What is fufuo and suya? We don't have it here.

Emmanuel：富富就是我们国家的主食，苏亚是另一种尼日利亚的美食。

Fufuo is our country's staple food, and suya is a famous dish in Nigeria.

赵：来尝尝北理工的美食吧！锡纸丘比鸡饭怎么样？这是清真食堂的一道名菜，鸡肉鲜嫩有嚼劲、微辣而不油腻，趁热喝一口汤，还能闻到浓郁的香味，而且营养丰富。

What about Tin-Foil Kewpie Chicken Combo? It is a famous dish here. The chicken is tender and chewy, slightly spicy without being greasy, and when you drink the hot soup, wow! Yummy and nutritious.

Emmanuel：还有什么菜？

Are there any other dishes?

赵：这儿还有老坛酸菜鱼泡饭、香浓牛肉汤、黄焖鸡米饭等，保管你吃一个月不重样。

There are Pickled Cabbage Fish Combo, beef soup, Braised Chicken Rice and so on. You can have different dishes for at least a month.

Emmanuel：太好了，我先要一份锡纸丘比鸡饭。看到这些菜让我胃口大开，中午要美美地大吃一顿了。

Great! I'm going to start with Tin Foil Kewpie Chicken Combo. These dishes give me a good appetite. Let's have a big lunch!

我不会用筷子
I Cannot Use Chopsticks

Emmanuel 点餐刷卡后，取到了他要的锡纸丘比鸡饭。但是他不会用筷子，恰好赵阳可以帮助他。

Emmanuel gets Kewpie Chicken Combo after ordering and swiping his campus card. But he cannot use chopsticks, and Zhao Yang helps him.

Emmanuel：饭菜真香啊！请问餐具在哪里呢？

It smells so good! How do I eat them?

赵：我帮你拿了筷子。

Here are your chopsticks.

Emmanuel：什么？筷子？我不会用筷子，我从来没用过筷子。

What? Chopsticks? I can't use chopsticks; I have never used them.

赵：你们国家用的是什么？

What do you use in your country?

Emmanuel：我们是用勺子和叉子来吃饭。

We use spoons and forks to eat.

赵：我来帮你。（赵阳给他示范怎样拿筷子）就这么简单，你试一试吧！

Ok, let me help you to use them. (Zhao Yang demonstrates how to use chopsticks) So easy, now it's your turn to try it!

Emmanuel：（试了几次）我还不会，太难了！

(After several attempts) I still can't. It's so difficult to manage!

赵: 没事，慢慢来。
It doesn't matter. Take your time!

Emmanuel: 那我暂时还是用叉子吧。
OK, I will. For the moment, I would rather use a fork.

赵: 好的，我让服务员给你叉子和勺子。
Okay, I will ask the attendant to get a set of fork and spoon for you.

Emmanuel: 真是太好吃了，它治好了我的思乡病，哈哈。
It really tastes great and cures my homesickness, ha-ha.

重点词汇
Keywords & expressions

富富	fufuo, fufu, foofoo
主食	staple food
筷子	chopsticks
思乡病	homesickness

1.2.3 北理工足球
BIT Soccer Team

足球季风

午饭后，Emmanuel 准备去图书馆。他和赵阳路过体育场时，看到很多人在踢足球。

After dinner, Emmanuel and Zhao Yang are going to the library. Passing by the soccer field, they see many people playing soccer.

Emmanuel: 快看，现在是有足球比赛吗？
Look, is there a soccer match now?

赵: 不，是足球运动员们在进行训练。
No, soccer players are training.

Emmanuel: 啊，知道了。这是哪儿的足球队？
Ah, I see. Which soccer team are they from?

赵: 这就是北京理工大学足球队，队员都是这儿在读的大学生。
Beijing Institute of Technology soccer team, and they are also full time students here.

Emmanuel: 快看，好漂亮的传球！
Look, what a nice pass!

赵: 射门！球进了！
Shoot! He made it goal!

Emmanuel: 太精彩了！
Miraculous!

Emmanuel: 他们是全日制的学生吗？踢得很专业呢！
Are they students? They look like professional players!

赵: 那当然了。咱们北理工足球队可是中国第一支全部以在校生为球员参加职业联赛的球队。
Of course, they are all professional soccer players and BIT students. Our BIT soccer team is the first team in China to participate in the

professional league with all players being university students.

Emmanuel：太酷了！北理工足球队是什么时候成立的？比赛成绩怎么样？

Cool! When was the soccer team established, and do they often participate in soccer matches?

赵：北理工足球队成立于2000年，到现在21年了，11次获得了中国大学生足球联赛的冠军*。它从2006年开始征战中国足球协会乙级联赛，已经两度升级进入甲级联赛。

The BIT soccer team was established in 2000 with a history of 21 years. The soccer team has been competing in the Chinese soccer Association Division Two League since 2006, and now participates in Chinese Football Association China League and the China University Football Association (CUFA). It has won the Chinese soccer Association Division Two League Championship once, and CUFA Championship for 11 times!

Emmanuel：哇，那可真是太厉害了！不过，他们每天训练和比赛这么忙，平时有时间学习吗？是不是不用参加考试了？

Wow, that's amazing! They are so occupied with training and matches every day. Do they have time to study, or do they need to take exams at all?

赵：当然需要考试了！对于他们来说，学生的身份是第一位的。他们比赛有压力，考试有更大的压力。比赛要赢，专业课考试也得通过。冠军要拿，学士学位、研究生学位也要拿。

Surely they do! Their identity of being a university student comes first. They are under pressure in competitions, and more pressure in examinations. They wish to win the game, and also to pass the CET-4 and CET-6 exams. They can win the championship, and they can also obtain the bachelor degree and postgraduate degrees.

篮球运动
Basketball Sports

篮球运动

Emmanuel：佩服！我也很喜欢足球和篮球，在尼日利亚我还参加过学校的运动队呢。

Amazing! I like both soccer and basketball games. I was the university's soccer team player in Nigeria.

赵：看你体格这么好，想必是和你喜爱运动分不开的。

That's why you are so fit! Sports help with body building!

Emmanuel：没错，谢谢。我要向这些大学生足球运动员学习，平衡好学习与兴趣！

Impressive! I like soccer very much, and I will learn from them to balance studying and personal interests.

这时，校园广播响起了一首歌曲，歌声中传唱着"我们是风，不被左右，我们是风，无法阻挡，北理工永远向前……"。

At this time, the campus radio sounded the song "We are the wind and cannot be swayed; we are the wind and cannot be stopped; BIT will always move forward"…

Emmanuel：哇，这首歌真好听！

Wow, the music sounds great!

赵：这首歌叫《足球季风》，是由北理工教师创作的足球队队歌，是北理工足球队拼搏向上精神的体现。

This song is called "Soccer Monsoon." It is the soccer team song composed by teachers of BIT. It embodies the spirit of BIT soccer team.

Emmanuel：嗯，旋律优美，朗朗上口。我也要学唱，下次比赛的时候为他们加油！

Well, the melody is beautiful and catchy. I'd like to learn it and cheer for them next time!

重点词汇

Keywords & expressions

中国足球协会甲级联赛　　Chinese Football Association China League
中国足球协会乙级联赛　　Chinese Football Association Division Two League
中国大学生足球联赛　　　China University Football Association (CUFA)

* 全国青少年校园足球联赛（大学组）男子超级冠军联赛，简称CUFA，是中国国内高校最高水平的足球联赛，前身为创办于2000年的大学生足球联赛。2021年6月，北京理工大学足球队第11次夺取这个赛事的桂冠。

China University Football Association, shortened as CUFA, is the top level football match of the Chinese universities. Previously it was known as the Chinese University Football League founded in 2000. In June 2021, BIT Soccer Team won the championship for the 11th time.

1.2.4 学在图书馆
Studying in the Library

如何查阅书籍

Emmanuel 到图书馆借阅专业书籍。他转了一圈，没能找到想要的书，就去找一位中国同学来帮忙。

Emmanuel wants to borrow a couple of professional books from the library. He looks around and can't find the book, then he comes up and asks a Chinese student for help.

Emmanuel：同学，你好！我是来自尼日利亚的留学生，我叫Emmanuel。你能帮助我吗？

Hello brother! I am Emmanuel from Nigeria. Could you do me a favor?

刘：好的，我叫刘建中，你有什么问题或者需要什

	me bāng zhù
	么 帮 助？
	Okay. I am Liu Jianzhong. What do you need?
Emmanuel：	wǒ shì dì yī cì dào tú shū guǎn zhǎo shū bù zhī dào zěn me zhǎo 我是第一次到图书馆找书，不知道怎么找。 It's my first time at the library and I don't know how to find the books I want.
刘：	nǐ xiǎng zhǎo de shū shū míng shì shén me 你想找的书，书名是什么？ No problem. What books do you want? Do you have their names?
Emmanuel：	bù hǎo yì sī wǒ méi yǒu tè dìng shū de míng zì wǒ zhǐ shì xiǎng fān kàn 不好意思，我没有特定书的名字。我只是想翻看 cái liào kē xué lèi de shū jí 材料科学类的书籍。 I'm sorry that I don't have a specific book's name. I just want to search for Materials Science books.
刘：	ó nǐ shì cái liào kē xué zhuān yè de ma 哦，你是材料科学专业的吗？ Oh, are you a materials science major?
Emmanuel：	shì de wǒ shì cái liào kē xué yǔ gōng chéng zhuān yè de bó shì yán jiū 是的，我是材料科学与工程专业的博士研究 shēng 生。 I'm a Ph. D. candidate in Materials Science and Engineering (MSE).
刘：	wā tài lì hài le cái liào xué shì běi lǐ gōng de yōu shì xué kē néng 哇，太厉害了。材料学是北理工的优势学科，能 zài běi lǐ gōng gōng dú zhè ge zhuān yè de bó shì xué wèi tǐng lì hài de 在北理工攻读这个专业的博士学位，挺厉害的 ne 呢。 Wow, awesome. MSE is one of the signature disciplines at BIT. Studying as a materials science doctorate candidate at BIT is really something.
Emmanuel：	xiè xiè nǐ guò jiǎng le 谢谢，你过奖了。

· 35 ·

Thank you. I am really flattered.

刘：啊，对了，自然科学类的书都在三层，材料科学类的书也在那里。在那边你可以用图书馆的电脑检索你想找的书：你只要输入书名或者关键词，很多书名和书架的位置就会呈现出来。你就可以按照所给的书架位置找到你想要的书。

Oh, by the way, books of science and technology are all on the third floor, where you can find materials science books. You can use computers there to index your desired books. You just need to enter the books' names or keywords and the books' list with locations will be displayed at once. Then you can find your desired books according to the given location.

Emmanuel：呃喔！你说的那些电脑是使用中文操作系统的吗？我的中文水平现在还不好，我怕看不懂。

Uh–oh! But isn't the computers' operating system Chinese? I'm still having a few problems in Chinese at present and I'm afraid I won't be able to understand.

刘：这个没问题，你把语言切换成英语就可以了。

That's not a problem at all. You can switch the language to English.

Emmanuel：那就好，谢谢你！

That's good! Thank you.

Emmanuel来到三层自然科学馆，还是找不着需要的书

第一章 留学北理共筑一梦

架位置。他又去找刘建中同学帮忙。

Emmanuel comes up to the science and technology zone on the third floor, and still cannot locate the book shelf he needs. Then, he turns to Liu Jianzhong for help again.

Emmanuel：刘建中同学，你好。这里的书太多了，我迷失位置了，找不着想要的书。

Hi, Liu Jianzhong. There are so many books inside that I can't find the book I want.

刘：你想要什么书？有书架位置吗？

What kind of book are you looking for? Have you got the location of the shelf?

Emmanuel：比如：我想找一本《新能源材料科学与应用技术》，从哪个书架上取？

How about *New energy materials science and Application technology*? Where can I find it?

刘：正好我想找的书也在那边，我们一起去找吧。

The book I'm looking for is also over there. Let's go searching together.

刘：我们到了。你需要的书应该在这个书架，我帮你找吧。

Here we are. The book you need should be on this shelf. I will take it for you.

刘建中在书架上很快取到了Emmanuel需要的图书。

Liu Jianzhong finds the book soon for Emmanuel.

下载电子书籍
Downloading Online E-books

如何下载电子书籍

Emmanuel：那除了纸质的书籍，还有电子版的吗？

Are there electronic books besides the hard copies?

刘：这是有的。因为很多同学习惯从互联网下载借阅相关的图书，所以图书馆也提供了丰富的电子书下载渠道。只要你的电脑配置了合适的浏览器，就可以下载浏览了。另外，图书馆还为本校师生提供了大量的免费文献查询服务。

Yes. Many students are used to downloading and borrowing electronic books from the Internet from many channels of the library. You can have easy access to these books with appropriate browsers. There is also abundant free literature searching service at the library.

Emmanuel：这对我的学习很有帮助。谢谢你啦！

This is very helpful. Thanks!

刘：不用客气。

Don't mention it.

Emmanuel 打开电脑，操作了一会儿，他又来找刘建中。

Emmanuel comes to Liu again after operating on the laptop for a while.

Emmanuel：刘同学，我想下载这篇文献，但是网页总是

第一章　留学北理共筑一梦

提示我没有权限下载，我不知道为什么。请问，你能帮我看一看怎么回事吗？

Excuse me, Liu! There is a note saying that I have no access to download this article. Could you please help me check it?

刘：　稍候，我来看看。

Just a second!

刘建中看了看Emmanuel电脑显示的信息和下载的问题。

After checking the information and download information...

刘：　哦，是这样的。下载文献需要登录校园网才可以的。

You need to log in on the campus net.

Emmanuel：明白了，那么怎么登录呢？

I see. How do I do that?

刘：　首先要把你的电脑无线网络，也就是Wi-Fi打开，连接到学校的无线信号。系统会提示你登录校园网，登录账号和初始密码都是你的学号，初次登录成功后，你就可以更改你的密码了。

First of all, You switch on the Wi-Fi and access the campus net with your student ID number as the login account and password. After the first time logging you can change the password.

Emmanuel：啊哈，好了，我已经登录上校园网了。

Aha! Done!

刘：　打开学校的官网首页，点击图书馆页面。进入图书馆主页后，再点击常用数据库，你就可以使用相应的数据库来检索、下载你需要的文献了。

Open the BIT website and click on the library page. Then, go into the database for the literature you need.

Emmanuel：北京理工大学的校园网下载文献真方便呀，速度也很快！

Wow, amazing speed and very convenient!

刘：是这样的。

Indeed.

寻找自习教室
Looking for a Study Lounge

寻找自习室

Emmanuel：刘同学，你平时除了来图书馆学习，一般还会去哪里上自习呢？

Liu, besides the library, where do you usually go for studying?

刘：在校园里，学生除了在图书馆阅览室学习，教学楼的空闲教室都可以用来自习，那里的环境一般都比较好，学习氛围也很好。当然，你也可以在宿舍里学习。

第一章 留学北理共筑一梦

You can use all the spare classrooms. Usually it's quieter there. But of course you can stay at dorm too.

Emmanuel：那我可能还是比较喜欢在教室里面学习。但是，我需要提前预约吗？

I prefer to study in the classrooms. Do I need to register?

刘：这个不用。只要是没有上课的教室，你都可以进去学习。在公共场合，不要大声喧哗和接打电话，不要影响到其他同学学习就可以了。

No. You just go in. Just keep quiet and don't take phone calls inside to disturb others please.

Emmanuel：你呢？你一般在哪儿学习？

Which place is your favorite?

刘：我经常去研究生教学楼上自习。因为研究生教学楼的教室多，总有没上课的教室可以利用，而且环境比较安静。

I use the Building for Graduate Students a lot. There are a lot of classrooms and very quiet places.

Emmanuel：其他的教学楼是怎么样的？

I wonder what other buildings are like?

刘：正好我这会儿有时间，要不我带你去逛逛，实地去参观一下北理工的教学楼吧。

I am free now. Why don't we go together to see some of them?

Emmanuel：太好了，谢谢刘同学。

Great! Thanks!

刘：那就走吧。
Let's go.

Emmanuel 和刘建中走出了图书馆。
Emmanuel and Liu walk out of the library.

刘：你到北理工这段时间感觉怎么样，喜不喜欢这里的生活？
How do you like BIT? Enjoy things here?

Emmanuel：非常喜欢，这里人人都友善。校园环境也很美，特别舒适，出乎意料得好。
Awesome! People here are very friendly. The environment in the campus is very good and comfortable. It's even better than I expected.

刘：你有这样的感受就很好。你也可以多交中国朋友，多了解中国的文化。
It's good for you to feel like this. You can also socialize with Chinese friends and get familiar with Chinese culture.

Emmanuel：嗯，你这个建议很对。可是我的汉语普通话还不行，没办法和中国同学们进行更多的交流。
Your advice is very good. My only concern is my Chinese will stop me from communicating with Chinese students.

刘：哦！如果你想练习汉语，我可以当你的语言伙伴，课余时间我们互相学习。
Oh! If you want to learn Chinese language, I can be your language

partner. we can learn together in our spare time.

Emmanuel：
tài hǎo le　　wǒ xiàn zài jiù xiǎng shuō hàn yǔ　　yī yǒu kōng wǒ jiù qù zhǎo
太好了，我现在就想说汉语，一有空我就去找
nǐ xué xí　xiè xiè nǐ yuàn yì bāng wǒ
你学习，谢谢你愿意帮我。

That's great, I really want to learn Chinese language. Whenever I have free time, I would like to talk with you. Thanks for being willing to help me to learn!

刘：
liú　　bié fàng zài xīn shàng　　méi shá
别放在心上，没啥。

Forget it. It was no big deal.

重点词汇

Keywords & expressions

图书馆	library
检索	index
操作系统	operating system, OS
互联网	the Internet
浏览器	browser
无线网络	Wi-Fi (Wireless Fidelity)
下载	download
登录	login
登录账号	login account
密码	password
文献	literature

1.2.5 便捷的快递
Convenient Express Delivery Service

校园里取快递

Emmanuel 和刘建中走在校园里。
Emmanuel and Liu Jianzhong are walking on campus.

Emmanuel：刘建中，请问小麦公社在哪儿？尼日利亚的亲戚给我邮寄了一些文件和日常用品，我去那儿取我的包裹。

Jianzhong, could you tell me where is the Wheat Commune? My cousin in Nigeria mailed me some documents and necessities. I need to get there and collect my package.

刘：沿着这条校园南路一直往西走，大约400米，向右拐到校园西路，再向北走100米，在道路的右手边就可以看到小麦公社了。

Go down the Campus South Road heading to the west for about 400 meters, then turn right to the Campus West Road; walk straight forward about 100 meters, and the Wheat Commune is on your right hand side of the road.

Emmanuel：好的，知道了。

刘：Emmanuel，在中国网上购物非常普及方便，日常用品不需要从你们尼日利亚寄来。在中

第一章 留学北理共筑一梦

国的互联网上有很多电子商务的购物平台，绝大多数的物品，如：日用品、食物、书籍、衣服、鞋和电子产品等都可以购买，你可以在不同购物平台比较后下单。快递非常便捷，通常第二天就能送到，还能减免运费。

Emmanuel, online shopping is very common and convenient in China, so necessities do not need to be sent from Nigeria. There are many e-commerce shopping online platforms in China. You can buy the vast majority of items online, such as: daily supplies, food, books, clothes, shoes and electronic devices. You can place an order after comparing on the different shopping platforms. Express delivery is fast which usually arrives on the next day after ordering and it can also reduce or waive shipping cost.

Emmanuel: 这太方便了。

Amazingly convenient!

刘: 为了保持大学校园的整洁和秩序，网购的包裹一般需要去南门外面取。

The online delivering parcels usually need to be collected out of the south gate for the clean and neat campus environment.

Emmanuel: 路远吗？

Is it far?

刘: 不远，走路大概10分钟。在前面的十字路口，左拐到体育馆西路，沿着体育馆向南走100

米，就到达南门了。

Not really, it's about a 10 minutes' walk. When you get at the first intersection along this road, turn left to the Gymnasium West Road, and walk ahead along the gym about 100 metres. You will get to the south gate.

Emmanuel：好的，我现在清楚了。

Okay, got it. Thank you!

刘：Emmanuel, 你有智能手机吗？

Emmanuel, have you got a smart phone?

Emmanuel：我有。

Yes, I have.

刘：只要把智能手机和借记卡或者信用卡绑定，你就可以实现快捷支付了。在中国，绝大多数的实体商店都可以通过扫码支付来购买商品，还可以购买门票和支付公交、地铁、出租车等出行费用。我给你演示一下。

You can buy anything by scanning barcodes with your smart phone at most stores in China or other purchases such as buying movie tickets, paying for bus or taxi fare and Metro Rail Transit (MRT). Just associate your smart phone to your debit or credit card. You have no more need to carry cash or bank card with you every day. I will show you.

刘建中和Emmanuel走进教学楼，找到一台自动贩卖机。刘建中选择了一瓶乌龙茶，掏出手机，用手机应用程序扫描机器上的二维码，马上就支付成功了，全程只用了几秒钟的时间。

Liu Jianzhong and Emmanuel walk into a teaching building, and find a vending machine where Liu buys a bottle of oolong tea by scanning a QR Code on the machine using an app software in his smart phone. Then, the payment proceeds immediately, taking only several seconds.

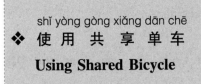
❖ 使用共享单车
Using Shared Bicycle

如何使用共享单车

走出教学楼，Emmanuel看见路边有很多不同颜色的自行车，便问刘建中：

Emmanuel sees many bicycles with different colors after going out of the teaching building, then he asks Liu Jianzhong,

Emmanuel：建中，在咱们校园里我发现很多同学和老师都骑着这种黄色或者蓝色的自行车，很方便。请问我在哪里可以买到？

Jianzhong, I found many students and teachers ride the bicycles in yellow or in blue on the campus. It is so convince! Could you tell me where I can buy one?

刘：这些自行车可不属于我们，也不用买。它们叫"共享单车"，也就是一种公共自行车。

Oh, these bicycles cannot belong to anyone, and cannot be bought.

They are shared bicycles, and that is a sort of public transportation.

Emmanuel：它原来是公共自行车啊。那怎样才能使用这种自行车呢？

So that it is a public bicycle. Then, how to use it?

刘：每辆共享单车上都有一个专属的二维码。如果你需要使用这辆自行车的话，扫描这个二维码，就可以打开这辆共享单车了。

Every shared bicycle has its own QR Code. You can scan the QR Code when you want to ride. Then, you will unlock the bicycle and use it.

Emmanuel：北理工的校园很大，骑上自行车，从宿舍到教室就能很快到了。你可以教教我怎么用吗？

The campus of BIT is really big. However, it will be soon from dormitory to classroom when I could ride. Could you tell me how to operate?

刘：没有问题，我来示范给你看。

No problem. I will show you.

刘建中掏出手机，用手机应用程序扫描共享单车上的二维码，车锁立刻自动打开了。

Liu Jianzhong takes out his smart phone, and uses app software in the phone to scan the QR Code on a shared bicycle. Then, the lock of the bicycle is opened automatically.

刘：当你骑行结束的时候，把车停放在规定的区域内，锁好车锁就可以了。需要支付的费用会自动出现在手机应用程序里，每次骑行的价格是很低廉的。

When you end your ride, stop in designated areas and lock the bicycle please. Riding fee to be paid will show in your app software, and it is really cheap!

Emmanuel：太神奇了，下次我也试一试。

Incredible! I will try it later.

刘：但是，你要保护好你的手机，不要丢失。

However, you should keep an eye on your smart phone and never lose it.

Emmanuel：好的，我会小心的。

OK, I'll be careful.

重点词汇

Keywords & expressions

网上购物	online shopping
电子商务	e-commerce
快递	express delivery
借记卡	debit card
信用卡	credit card
应用程序	app（application）
扫码	scan barcodes
二维码	QR（Quick Response）Code

1.2.6 交往礼节 (jiāo wǎng lǐ jié)
Social Etiquette

周末的上午，Emmanuel 和刘建中正在练习中文会话，留学生中心的陈老师敲门进来。

Emmanuel and Liu Jianzhong are practicing Chinese conversation on a weekend morning. Ms. Chen from the Office of International Students knocks at the door and comes in.

陈：Emmanuel，你好。刘建中，你好。
Hello, Emmanuel. Hello, Liu Jianzhong.

刘：陈老师，您好。
Ninhao, Ms. Chen.

Emmanuel：陈老师，你好。你找我，有什么事吗？
Nihao, Ms. Chen. What's up?

陈：Emmanuel，从学籍系统中看到今天是你的生日，留学生中心特意为你准备了一份礼物，祝你生日快乐！
Emmanuel, the Student Registering System shows that today is your birthday, and the Office of International Students specially prepares a gift for you and wishes you happy birthday!

刘：Emmanuel，生日快乐！
Happy birthday to you, Emmanuel!

第一章　留学北理共筑一梦

Emmanuel：（大笑起来）我都忘了今天是我的生日。我太高兴了！谢谢陈老师！谢谢建中！

(Laughed heartily) I have totally forgot it is my birthday. That's a happy surprise! Thank you, Ms. Chen! Thank you, Jianzhong!

Emmanuel 一接到礼物，就准备打开。

Emmanuel starts to open the present as soon as he receives it.

刘：嘿！Emmanuel，别着急打开！

Hey! Emmanuel, don't open it in such a hurry!

Emmanuel：怎么了？为什么不能打开？

What's wrong? Why shouldn't I open it?

刘：你知道吗，在中国文化中，当你收礼物的时候，一般要等客人离开以后才打开，这样是礼貌的。

You know what, in Chinese culture, when you receive a gift, you don't open it in front of the gift giver but wait till they leave. We consider, it is more polite this way.

Emmanuel：是吗？在尼日利亚，收到礼物可以直接拆开。这样，送礼物的人会根据你的反应来判断你是否喜欢它，这很正常。

Really? when we receive a gift in Nigeria, we open it right away so the gift giver gets to know whether you like it or not.

刘：这就是文化差异。在中国如果你当时就打开礼物，送给你礼物的人或者其他客人会感觉到尴尬的。

This must be cultural difference. In Chinese culture, opening the gift immediately might make us embarrassed.

Emmanuel: 好的，我明白了。以后我会注意的。

Okay, I understand. I won't do that next time.

Emmanuel: 建中，刚才你为什么说"您好"？

Jianzhong, why did you say *ninhao* just now?

刘： 你和您，只是语意上的细微差别。在同辈、同学之间，我们提到对方，常常直接用"你"。"您"是敬语，对于年龄偏大的长辈、或者身份较高的老师，出于尊重的原因，我们用"您"来称呼。

It's just a linguistic nuance between *ni* and *nin*. When we talk to friends, peers or classmates, we use *ni* directly. While *nin* is honorific. For reasons of respect, we use *nin* call people like elders or teachers.

Emmanuel: 我又学到了新知识。建中，谢谢你！

I learned something new. Jianzhong, *xiexie ni*!

Emmanuel: 陈老师，谢谢您！

Ms. Chen, *Xiexie nin*!

陈： 不客气，祝你在北理工生活愉快，学有所成！

It's a pleasure. Wish you happy staying here and success in your studies in BIT!

第一章 留学北理共筑一梦

重点词汇
Keywords & expressions

社交礼仪	social etiquette
礼物	gift/present
生日快乐	happy birthday
尴尬	embarrass
细微差别	nuance

1.2.7 北理工国际文化节
BIT International Culture Festival

校园文化活动

Emmanuel 在宿舍里看书，他的巴基斯坦同学 Naveed 来找他。

Emmanuel is reading in the dormitory, and his Pakistani friend Naveed comes to him.

Naveed：嗨，Emmanuel，你在做什么？
Hi, Emmanuel, what are you doing?

Emmanuel：我在看书呀，你有什么计划？
I am studying and reading. What are you up to?

Naveed：今天北理工在校园里举办露天的国际文化节，

我们一起去参加吧。
The outdoor International Culture Festival of BIT is on campus today. Let's go and visit together.

Emmanuel：好啊！我还不知道这个消息。
Good! I don't know the news yet.

北理工国际文化节
International Culture Festival of BIT

Emmanuel 和 Naveed 来到中心教学楼前面，主舞台就设置在这里。来自40多个国家的500余名留学生都汇集到这儿，气氛隆重热闹。沿着中心花园两侧，还搭建了40多个国家展台，展示各个国家的特色文化和民族风情。

Emmanuel and Naveed come to the front of the central building, where a big stage is set. More than 500 international students from about 40 countries are gathering there with cheerful and ceremonious atmosphere. More than 40 country booths have been set up along the sides of campus central garden to display the unique culture and customs of each country.

第一章 留学北理共筑一梦

Naveed 首先来到巴基斯坦展区，他看到了一位美丽的女士正在给参观的同学手绘汉娜。Naveed 上前和她打招呼。

Naveed comes to Pakistan Exhibition booth. He sees a pretty lady hand-painting the Henna pattern for other visiting students. Naveed goes up and says hello to her.

Naveed：你好！我是Naveed Muhammad，今年刚从巴基斯坦来到北理工，在材料学院攻读博士学位。

Hello! My name is Naveed Muhammad and I have just arrived BIT from Pakistan this year. Now, I am studying for Ph. D. in the school of Materials Science and Engineering(MSE).

Attia：你好！我是Attia Batool，我也是在材料学院攻读博士学位。

Hello! I am Attia Batool, and I am studying for Ph. D. in the school of MSE, too.

Naveed：太巧了！我们既是同乡又是同学，以后要经常联系，一起研究解决学术上的难题，共同取得进步啊。

What a happy coincidence! Since we are both town fellows and schoolmates, we should keep in tight touch, discussing academic problems constantly and making progress together.

Attia：好啊。在那边还有几位材料学院的新同学。

All right. There are some new students from School of MSE there.

Naveed： 我去找他们。Attia，回头见。
I will look for them. Attia, see you around.

Attia： 再见，Naveed。
See you soon, Naveed!

Emmanuel 在互动游戏区认识了几位来材料学院攻读博士学位的新同学，他们是：Naeem, Tahir, Adnan 和 Souleymen。他们欣赏了各民族的传统服饰，品尝了多国"舌尖上的美食"。主舞台上精彩的节目正好戏连台，有气势恢宏的中国功夫、热情奔放的非洲舞蹈、婉转动听的歌曲演唱、异彩纷呈的民族乐器演奏以及趣味横生的抖空竹表演，引得台下叫好声不断。入夜时分，中心花园里华灯璀璨，是一片欢声笑语的海洋。各国的留学生依然兴致高昂，久久不愿散去。

Emmanuel meets with several new Ph. D. candidate students Naeem, Tahir, Adnan and Souleymen from School of MSE at the interactive games zone. They enjoy the traditional costumes of various ethnics, taste the delicious food from different countries. At that time, the programs start on the main stage with magnificent Chinese kung fu, passionate African dances, melodious songs singing, colorful folk instrument playing and funny diabolo performance, triggering a roar of cheers from the audience. In the evening with all lights shining, there is still a sea of joy and laughter in the campus central garden. International students are still in high spirits, they would not leave the grand gala.

Emmanuel: 今天过得太开心了，真是令人难忘的一天！

So much fun today, and it is full of exciting memories and rewarding experiences!

Naveed: 北理工是一所多姿多彩，充满活力与动感的大学。

BIT is a university with lots of diversity, vitality and dynamism.

Emmanuel: 嗯，北京理工大学太棒了，这片美丽的校园就是我们的"幸福园"！

Quite thrilling! The beautiful campus is our Happiness Garden!

北理工"幸福园"
BIT Happiness Garden

Keywords & expressions

国际文化节	International Culture Festival
巴基斯坦	Pakistan
汉娜	Henna pattern
中国功夫	Chinese kung fu
空竹	Diabolo/Chinese yo-yo

第二章 材以养德，料以治学
STUDYING FINE MATERIALS FOR KNOWLEDGE AND VIRTUE

2.1 材料学院概述
Overview of the School of MSE

材料学院概述

Emmanuel 在北京理工大学报到注册以后，迫切想要了解材料学院的情况。他来到五号教学楼内的学院办公室，研究生干事罗老师接待了他。

Emmanuel is eager to know more about the School of Materials Science and Engineering（MSE）when he comes to Beijing Institute and Technology. He comes to the School's Administrative Office at the No. 5 Teaching Building. Ms. Luo who is in charge of postgraduate academic affairs greets him.

Emmanuel：罗老师，您好，我是Emmanuel。我想多知道一些材料学院的讯息。

Hello, Ms. Luo. I want to know more information about School of MSE.

罗：Emmanuel，你好。材料学院由六个专业组成，分别是：材料化学、材料成型与控制工程、高分子材料与工程、电子封装技术、材料科学与工程以及新能源材料与器件。

Hello, Emmanuel. The School of MSE consists of six programs. They are materials chemistry, material forming and control engineering, polymer materials and engineering, electronic packaging technology, materials science and engineering, and new energy materials and devices.

Emmanuel：您能介绍一下每个专业的基本情况吗？

Could you please be more specific about each of the department?

罗：材料化学专业面向国民经济建设，开展光电信息、新能源、医工融合等前沿交叉领域的新材料研究，引领国家科研重大需求的最新生长点。

The program of materials chemistry aims at promoting the development of national economy by carrying out new materials research on leading interdisciplinary fields of photoelectric information, new energy, the integration of engineering and medicine, etc., and catering for the latest demands of major national scientific research.

材料成型与控制工程专业是解决材料的成型工艺和成型设备开发，研究各种模具以及工装设计等相关的基础理论与优化方法。

The program of material forming and control engineering is engaged in developing material molding process and molding equipment, as well as various mold and tooling design and other related fundamental theory and optimization methods.

高分子材料与工程专业主要研究石油化工、高分子功能材料及特种高分子复合材料。

The program of polymer materials and engineering mainly focuses on the research on petrochemicals, polymer functional materials and special polymer composite materials.

电子封装技术专业研究微电子器件的制造工艺和先进封装技术。

The program of electronic packaging technology is studying on the manufacturing and advanced packaging technology of microelectronic devices.

材料科学与工程专业主要研究金属材料和无机非金属材料的基础理论，从事金属材料和无机材料的环境冲击性能、新工艺开发、质量控制等研究工作。

The program of materials science and engineering mainly focuses on the research on theoretical basis of metal and inorganic non-metallic materials, and is mainly engaged in the fundamental research of metal and inorganic non-metallic materials, environmental impact properties, new process development, quality control, etc.

新能源材料与器件专业研发各种新能源材料，应用于新型、可再充电的二次电池，以及二次电池的智能制造、退役电池回收再利用的新技术。

The program of new energy materials and devices conducts research on all kinds of new secondary batteries, and the new technology to reduce adverse environmental impacts during battery manufacturing and recycling of spent battery.

材料学院的目标是培养材料科学与工程学科领域不同层次上的专业人才，并从事各种高新材料的科学理论和前沿技术的探索性研究。

The goal of MSE is to cultivate scientific and technical talents at different levels in the field of materials science and engineering, and it also engages in the fundamental, development and application research of various novel and advanced materials.

Emmanuel：获得了材料学的学位，我可以去从事哪些行业的工作？

What kind of job can I take after obtaining the degree of materials science?

罗：我们材料学院的毕业生可以从事材料学科相关领域的学术探索、技术研发、销售支持、科技金融和科技管理等工作。他们很多都进入了巴斯夫股份公司、陶氏化学公司、宝洁公司等世界500强企业；中国航天集团、中国石化集团、中国北方工业集团、北京汽车集团等中国的大型国有企事业单位；国内外的知名大学以及研究院所；各级政府机关等。他们都有着良好的就业前景。

The alumni of School of MSE work in varied lines including scientific research, technology development, sales support, Fintech and management—all related to high-tech materials. Many of our graduates have been recruited by Fortune Global 500 companies such as BASF SE, Dow Chemical Company, P&G Company, and China's large state-owned enterprises such as China Aerospace Science and Technology Corporation(CASC), Sinopec Group, China North Industries Group Corporation Limited(NORINCO Group), Beijing Automotive Industry Corporation(BAIC Group). Some of them go to work at domestic and overseas first-rate universities, research institutes and government agencies at all levels.

Emmanuel：材料学院有哪些特色的科研方向呢？

What are the feature research areas in the School of MSE?

罗：有低维纳米材料及量子点材料、功能高分子材料、阻燃材料、含能材料、先进材料成型理论与技术、材料表面工程等的研究。

Different research directions include low-dimensional and quantum dot-based nano-materials, functional polymers, flame retardant materials, energetic materials, forming theory and technology for advanced materials, and material surface engineering.

Emmanuel：您能分别介绍一下吗？我对这些研究都很感兴趣。

Could you tell me in details? I am very interested in these topics.

罗：低维纳米材料及量子点材料包括各种零维、一维、二维的光、电、磁纳米材料的制备与性能，特别是高性能半导体纳米材料的构建及其在发光显示、太阳能电池、吸透波等领域的应用。

Research on low-dimensional and quantum dot-based nano-materials includes the preparation techniques and research on optical, electrical, and magnetic properties of various zero-dimensional, one-dimensional, two-dimensional nano-materials, especially the construction of high-performance semiconductor nano-materials and their application in luminescence, solar cells, transmission and absorption of microwave.

功能高分子材料主要包括光电功能高分子材料、阻燃材料、生物医用材料及天然高分子材料等。

Research on functional polymer materials mainly includes photoelectric functional polymer materials, flame-retardant materials, biomedical materials, and natural polymers.

含能材料主要包括高能量密度聚合物、纳米含能材料、功能含能助剂的分子结构设计、合成与制备工艺；高性能固体推进剂及成型工艺与应用；包覆层与绝热层材料技术等。

Research on energetic materials includes molecular design, synthesis and preparation of high energy density polymers, nano-energetic materials, functional energizer agents, high performance solid propellants and their molding process and application, as well as cladding and insulation layer materials technology.

先进材料成型理论与技术主要研究材料的各种先进加工技术、前沿成型理论与工程应用、加工成型及材料组织与性能的关系;材料加工成型的仿真技术等。

Research on advanced material forming theory and technology includes various advanced processing and forming theories and engineering applications, the relationship between material processing forming and material structure and performance, numerical simulation and simulation technology of material processing forming.

材料表面工程主要包括特种涂层结构—功能一体的优化设计与材料合成、涂层制备全过程的数值模拟与性能预测;表面涂层加工以及微结构控制;涂层性能测试与表征等。

Research on materials surface engineering includes optimized design of the special surface coating structure and functional integration, complete simulation and performance prediction of the coating preparation process, surface coating processing and micro structural control, coating performance testing and characterization.

Emmanuel：这些研究方向听起来太吸引人了,您能再给我详细介绍它们的研究内容吗?

The names of these studies sound so attractive. Could you please give me a bit more details?

罗：我们学院有一位翟教授，很和善，他所在的课题组也有外籍留学生在攻读博士学位。可以让翟教授给你们介绍材料学院的科研内容。

I would like to introduce you to Professor Zhai at our school. He is nice. There are some international students studying for Ph. D. at his research group of Prof. Zhai. I think Prof. Zhai will be able to give you more professional information about School of MSE.

Emmanuel：太好了！谢谢罗老师！

That's great! Thank you, Ms. Luo!

罗老师拨通了翟教授的办公室电话。

Ms. Luo dials Prof. Zhai's office phone number.

罗：翟老师，您好。今年我们学院新报到一批外籍留学生，他们很希望了解学院的科研内容。您有空给他们介绍一下吗？

Hello, Prof. Zhai. A group of new international students have enrolled in our school this year, and they are all eager to know about the research at our school. Do you have time to give them an introduction?

翟：好的，罗老师。下周一上午，请他们来我的办公室，我带领他们参观材料学院，并讲解学院的科研方向。

Okay, Ms. Luo. Let them come to my office next Monday morning. I will show them around the school of MSE, and introduce the scientific research directions to them.

罗：辛苦翟老师了！
That's very kind of you!

翟：没关系，这是应该的。
It's my pleasure.

重点词汇
Keywords & expressions

材料化学	materials chemistry
材料成型与控制工程	material forming and control engineering
成型	forming, molding
高分子	polymer
复合材料	composite materials
电子封装技术	electronic packaging technology
新能源材料与器件	new energy materials and devices
金属材料	metal materials
无机材料	inorganic materials
环境冲击性能	environmental impact properties
可再充电的	rechargeable
二次电池	secondary battery
退役电池	spent battery
回收再利用	recycling
世界500强	Fortune Global 500
低维	low-dimensional
纳米材料	nano-materials
量子点	quantum dots

半导体	semiconductor
阻燃材料	flame retardant materials
含能材料	energetic materials
材料表面工程	material surface engineering
太阳能电池	solar cell
推进剂	propellant
包覆层	cladding
绝热层	insulation layer
数值模拟	numerical simulation

cái liào xué yuàn wǔ hào lóu
材料学院五号楼
Building NO. 5, School of MSE

　　　　　　　cóng xué yuàn bàn gōng shì chū lái hòu　rèn zhēn guān kàn yuè dú lóu nèi
　　Emmanuel 从 学 院 办 公 室 出 来 后，认 真 观 看 阅 读 楼 内
jiè shào gè gè shí yàn shì de qiáng bào　zhè shí　yī wèi nǚ tóng xué jīng guò tā
介 绍 各 个 实 验 室 的 墙 报。这 时，一 位 女 同 学 经 过 他，
　　　　jiào zhù le tā
Emmanuel 叫 住 了 她。

　　When Emmanuel is reading the posters on the wall along the corridor

第二章 材以养德，料以治学

introducing each laboratory after he gets out of the school office, a female student passes by. Emmanuel comes up and talks to her.

Emmanuel：同学，你好。我是Emmanuel，来自尼日利亚。请问，你是材料学院的学生吗？

Hello! My name is Emmanuel from Nigeria. Excuse me, are you a student at School of MSE?

刘：是呀，我是材料学院的博士研究生。我叫刘钰。Emmanuel，你好。

Yes, I am Liu Yu, a doctoral candidate in MSE. Hello, Emmanuel!

Emmanuel：刘同学，我刚来到材料学院，想知道怎么在实验室里开展科学研究？

Miss Liu, I just came to the School of MSE. I wonder how to do the scientific research in the laboratory.

刘：那我要先考考你的基础知识。什么是材料科学与工程？

I am going to give you a quiz on your basic knowledge firstly. What is the materials science and engineering (MSE)?

Emmanuel：让我想想……材料科学与工程是通过深入理解组分-结构、合成-工艺、性质、使用效能这四个基本要素之间的相互关系来发明新材料和改进提高现有材料的一个跨学科专业。把四要素连接起来，就构成了材料科学与工程的四面体模型。

Let me see... Materials science and engineering (MSE) is an interdisciplinary field concerned with inventing new materials and improving previously known materials by developing a deeper understanding on the relationship among four basic elements: composition-structure, synthesis-process, property and performance. These four basic elements constitute a MSE tetrahedron model.

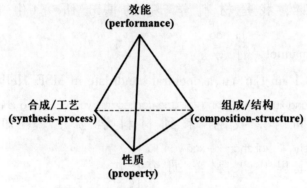

材料科学与工程四面体
MSE Tetrahedron Model

刘：嗯，那你再说说，材料科学与工程对现代社会发展有什么影响？

Well, what impact does MSE have on the development of modern society?

Emmanuel：材料科学与工程是二十一世纪国民经济和工业生产的重要支柱，也是航天、航空、信息、国防等高新技术进步的基础。随着人类文明的发展，对新材料的要求不断提高，由直接使用天然材料转化为加工制作新材料，再发展为研制

第二章 材以养德，料以治学

合成新材料。近现代以来，在科学技术的推动下，高效能的新材料不断涌现，传统材料的性能也得到了改善，力求满足各方面的需求。因此，材料科学与工程已成为科技发展的基础以及工业生产的支柱。

MSE plays an important support role for the development of the national economy and for high-tech advancement in aerospace, aviation, information technology, and national defense. With the development of human civilization and production capacity, the requirements for new materials are constantly increasing. Therefore, MSE begins from collecting natural materials, then to machining and manufacturing, and now develops to synthesis and preparation of materials. Under the impetus of modern science and technology, the variety of new materials with different properties are emerging and the performance of raw materials is improved so as to meet various requirements. Therefore, MSE has become the basis of scientific and technological development as well as the pillar of industrial production.

刘：嗯，还算不错。

Well, not bad.

刘：材料学院为提高工作质量和效率，搭建了高水平的科研平台。你正观看的这个"低维功能材料实验室"就隶属于"结构可控先进功能材料与绿色应用北京市重点实验室"。

School of MSE established high-level research platforms to improve work quality and efficiency. The lab we are at now is called Low-dimensional Functional Materials Laboratory and it belongs to Beijing Key Laboratory of Construction Controlled Advanced Functional Materials and Green Application.

Emmanuel：低维功能材料实验室有几位老师？
How many faculties are there at the Low-dimensional Functional Materials Laboratory?

刘：有六位老师。材料学院按照课题组为基本单位开展科研活动。课题组内由一位资深教授担任学术领头人，由其他几名教授、副教授、讲师和在实验室进行科研工作的博士生、硕士生、本科生共同组成。曹教授是"低维功能材料实验室"的学术领头人，我就在这个实验室里工作。
There are six full time faculties. The school of MSE carries out scientific research activities with research groups as the basic units. A senior professor acts as the principal investigator (PI) in the group, and other professors, associate professors, lecturers and doctoral students, graduates and undergraduate students constitute the research group together. Prof. Cao is PI in Low-dimensional Functional Materials Laboratory, and I also work in it.

Emmanuel：我也希望能进入低维功能材料实验室，请你以后多帮助我。
I wish I could join in the Low-dimensional Functional Materials Laboratory. Please give me some help.

刘：没问题，欢迎你加入我们课题组。

No problem. You are welcome to join us!

重点词汇
Keywords & expressions

实验室	laboratory, lab
墙报	poster
组分－结构	composition-structure
合成－工艺	synthesis-process
性质	property
使用效能	performance
要素	basic element
四面体模型	tetrahedron model
低维功能材料	low-dimensional functional materials
学术领头人	principal investigator, PI

2.2 参观材料学院
Visiting the School of MSE

参观材料学院实验室

星期一的上午，阳光明媚。Emmanuel、Naveed、Naeem、Tahir、Adnan、Souleymen 和 Attia 几位外籍留学生来到翟教授的办公室，翟教授已经在办公室等他们了。

On a sunny Monday morning, international students Emmanuel, Naveed, Naeem, Tahir, Adnan, Souleymen and Attia come to Prof. Zhai's Office. Prof. Zhai is waiting for them.

Emmanuel: 翟教授，早上好。

Good morning, Prof. Zhai.

翟: 早上好。很高兴见到大家。

Good morning. Nice to see you all.

翟: 看到你们，让我想起了课题组以前的一位巴基斯坦学生。他叫 Muhammad Tahir，于2011年入学，并在曹教授的指导下来我们实验室进行科研工作。他在2015年毕业，并且获得了博士学位。

You remind me of a former Pakistani student in our research group. His name is Muhammad Tahir. He was enrolled in 2011 and carried out scientific research under the guidance of Prof. Cao in our laboratory. He obtained Ph. D. degree in 2015.

Naveed: 我们都知道他。这儿还有一个好消息。Tahir 回国以后，因为在材料科学的研究领域不断取得成就，他在2018年获得了"阿卜杜勒·萨拉姆奖"*。这是在巴基斯坦有着很高声誉的学术奖项。

We all heard of him. Here is another piece of good news. Tahir received the Abdus Salam Award from the Academy of Sciences of Pakistan and the Academy of Sciences for Developing Countries in 2018 for his continuous achievements in the field of MSE. It's a prestigious award in Pakistan.

翟: 太好了！祝贺Tahir! 我会把这个好消息告诉曹教

第二章 材以养德，料以治学

授，他一定很高兴。

Wonderful! Congratulations! Prof. Cao would be very happy to hear about that.

Tahir： 是的。他是我们的榜样。

Exactly. He is our role model.

Naeem： 我们这儿还有一位Tahir。

We have another Tahir here.

大家把Tahir推到前面，Tahir腼腆地笑了。

They pushed Tahir to the front, who has a shy smile on the face.

翟： 你们俩人的名字是一模一样吗？

Do you both have the same name?

Tahir： 是的。

Yes, exactly.

翟： 那希望你也取得和先前的Tahir一样的好成绩。

Amazing! Then hope you get the same achivement too!

Tahir： 谢谢翟教授！我会努力工作的！

Thank you, Prof. Zhai! I will work hard!

翟： 我也有好消息要告诉你们。北理工材料科学的学科影响力在国际上稳步提升。自2017年以来的QS世界大学学科排名中，北理工材料学科一直稳居全球前100名；在2020年进入ESI世界学科排名前1‰的行列；同时，在2020年US news世界大学

· 75 ·

学科排名中位列第87名。

I also have good news for you. The influence MSE School at BIT is steadily increasing in the academia. BIT MSE ranked the top 100 at QS World University Rankings by Subject since 2017 and 2018. It also entered top 1‰ in 2020 ESI Subject Ranking, and ranked 87th in the disciplines of the 2020 US News World University Rankings.

Emmanuel：我们来到北理工材料学院，真的是来对了地方。

The school of MSE in BIT is exactly the place that we want to come to.

翟：我们所在的5号教学楼就是材料学院的总部和主要科研的所在地。此外，还有一些实验室分散在中关村校区的各个实验楼里。现在我就带你们参观5号楼里的实验室。我们在楼道里遇到那些衣着朴素、若有所思的路人可能就是像爱因斯坦那样身怀绝学的大教授。

The No. 5 Building where we are at now is the main research base of the School of MSE. Besides, some laboratories are scattered in other buildings of Zhongguancun campus. Now, I'll show you around the laboratories of MSE in No. 5 Building. The passers-by, plain in clothing, deep in thought wandering in the corridor, maybe are Einstein-like professors.

Adnan：哇喔！

Wow!

第二章 材以养德，料以治学

众人首先来到材料学院的院长办公室。

They come to the Dean's Office at the first stop.

翟： 庞院长，您好。这些是今年来我们学院学习的外籍留学生们。（转向留学生们）这是庞院长，庞院长是材料学院的领头羊。

Hello, Professor Pang. They are new international students studying in our school this year. (Turning to the students) This is the Dean, Professor Pang, the head of the school of MSE.

Emmanuel： 庞院长，您好。

How do you do? Dean Pang.

庞： 大家好，很高兴见到你们！

How do you do? Very glad to meet you!

翟： 庞院长，留学生们想了解我们学院的学科发展，请您给他们介绍一下。

Professor Pang, they would like to know about the recent development of research at our school.

庞： 好呀！在创新驱动的发展战略下，北京理工大学的材料科学家们面向工业进步的需求，正在进行尖端的科学研究，不断开发出新的工程制造技术。

Okay! With an innovation-driven development strategy, material scientists at Beijing Institute of Technology are conducting cutting-edge research and developing novel techniques to find solutions for

· 77 ·

industrial advancement.

庞: 我们通过研究新材料的力学、电学、光学、热学和磁学性质，专注于为材料工程提供全新的理念、技术和制备方法。

We focus on design concepts, preparation methods, and new techniques for material engineering by studying the mechanical, electrical, optical, thermal, and magnetic properties of new materials.

庞: 为了构建和提升材料领域影响力的框架，我们的目标是采用颠覆性的技术在未来产业中表达和满足对新材料的需求。

In order to construct a framework for boosting material impact, we aim for developing disruptive technologies that address new material needs in emerging industries.

Souleymen: 庞院长，材料学院有多少教授有资质作为导师，指导外籍留学生攻读博士学位？

Dean Pang, how many professors have the qualification to guide international students studying for Ph. D?

庞: 现在有70多名教授有这样的资质。他们都是学术精深、师德高尚的导师。正是这些教授们的辛勤工作才造就了材料学院今天的成绩。

More than 70 professors do. All of them are supervisors with profound academic knowledge and noble ethics. It is these professors' hard work that has led to the present achievements of the School of MSE.

第二章 材以养德，料以治学

Naveed： 庞院长，您刚刚讲的先进材料研究，可以给我们举个例子吗？

Dean Pang, could you give us an example about the advanced research you mentioned?

庞： 我的团队发展了一个新理念，采用特殊方法合成出了一种笼型的金属有机框架材料。它是一种易于膨胀的多孔含能材料，具有独特的分子结构。与常规高能材料相比，它既能提供更高的热能，又能降低敏感度。我们希望激发出这种新材料的极限潜能。这种理念为下一代高能量密度材料的设计和合成提供了新的思路。

One of our group has developed the concept of cage-type metal-organic frameworks (MOFs), which are porous materials pliable to expansion. Compared with conventional energetic materials, they have improved thermal energy and reduced sensitivity. We want to expand the potential limits of new materials with the unique molecules synthetized with a special method. This unique concept has shed light on the design and synthesis of next-generation high-energy-density materials.

Tahir： 庞院长，请问这项研究有什么意义呢？

Dean Pang, what is the significance of this reasearch?

庞： 我们的研究成果可以应用于工业领域，而且从理论上强化了我们对能量稳定性和物质结构之间关系的深入理解。

Our research not only works for industrial applications, but also contributes to improve our understanding of the relationship between energy, stability and material structures.

翟：谢谢庞院长的介绍。下一站，我们去拜访材料学院两位久负盛名的科学家，王教授和才教授。他们的研究方向是金属材料。

Thanks for your time, Dean. Next stop, we will visit two renowned scientists, Prof. Wang and Prof. Cai. They both do research on metal.

众人：庞院长，再见。

Goodbye, Dean Pang.

庞：同学们，再见。

See you later, everyone.

众人来到了王教授和才教授的实验室。

The crowd come to Professor Wang and Professor Cai's laboratory

翟：王教授最近对高熵合金的设计有了新颖的想法。

Prof. Wang has got a novel idea on the design of high-entropy alloys (HEAs) recently.

Naeem：王教授，您好。请问什么是高熵合金？

Hello, Prof. Wang. What is the high-entropy alloy?

王：高熵合金是至少四种或四种以上约略等量的金属形成的合金，这种独特的合金设计理

第二章 材以养德，料以治学

念体现出多种元素的协同效应。高熵合金具有很好的力学性能，在很多应用场合都是具有潜力的竞争材料。要扩展它的用途，还需要获得同时具有高密度、超高强度和延展性的高熵合金。

High entropy alloys (HEAs) are alloys consisting of at least four or more metals with approximately equal molar quantities. The unique alloy design concept reflects the synergistic effect of multiple metal elements. HEAs are promising candidates for many new applications, given their superior mechanical properties. To expand their application, a new strategy to design high density, ultra-high strength and ductile HEAs is needed.

Naeem: 您是怎么来设计高熵合金的呢？

How do you design HEAs?

王： 近期，高熵合金吸引全球材料研究人员的关注，但是强度的大小限制了它们在工业上的应用。我们发现有序－无序交替的调幅相纳米结构可以用来提高材料的强度，于是提出了一种全新的纳米强化机制。设计思想的关键是，在分离出足够多的强化相以后，形成一个高熵固溶体的基体，就能够在保持材料延展性的同时提高合金的强度了。

HEAs have drawn lots of attention globally these days. But limits on strength have restricted their industrial applications. The key to my group's design is forming a high-entropy solid-solution matrix after separating out adequate strengthening phases.

Adnan: 王教授，请问这种高熵合金有什么用途呢？

What is the application of the HEAs, Prof. Wang?

王: 由于多重元素的协同作用，这种高熵合金还具有更强的耐腐蚀性和抗氧化性，可以作为一种理想的防护涂层材料。

My group designed a nano structure with a new mechanism to enhance alloy strength while maintaining its ductility. We found that the modulated ordered-disordered nano structure contributes to the elevated strength. With the synergistic effect of multiple elements, the alloy is also more resistant to corrosion and oxidation, making it ideal for protective coatings.

Adnan: 高熵合金的研究前景是什么？

What are the prospects for the HEAs research?

王: 这个领域未来的趋势将从合金的高熵组成转向高熵相的研究。

The future trend in this field will move from high-entropy alloys to high-entropy phases.

翟: 才教授率先开发了轻质非晶复合材料，以及具有更好的承载能力和保护能力的金属-陶瓷复合材料。

Prof. Cai has taken the lead in developing technologies for lightweight non-crystalline composites and metal-ceramic composite materials with improved load-bearing and protective capacities.

才： 高通量设计、制备和测量，结合金属和非金属轻量级材料工程，对于结构和功能的集成至关重要。同时，我们正在开发材料基因组工程技术，将材料的结构、功能和能量的数据整合到一起，并且以此建立了国家新材料数据中心，为国内和国际同行提供各种类型的材料数据服务。

High-throughput design, preparation and measurement combined with metallic/non-metallic lightweight material engineering are essential for the integration of structure and function. We are exploring material genome engineering technologies to integrate structural, functional, and energetic materials by building a national new material data center to serve domestic and international materials science peers.

众人接着又去拜访了吴教授和杨教授。

Then, they go on to visit Prof. Wu and Prof. Yang.

翟： 吴教授的研究方向是新能源材料包括二次充放电电池材料和整体组件。吴教授因他在电池技术方面出色的工作而获得了许多国内和国际的重要奖项，包括：国际电池协会研究奖和

2021储能杰出贡献奖。

Prof. Wu's research is on new energy materials including secondary rechargeable battery materials and battery integral components. Prof. Wu has won many national and international awards for his outstanding work on battery technologies, including International Battery Association(IBA)'s Research Award and Outstanding Contribution to Energy Storage Award 2021.

吴：我的团队提出了采用轻元素、多电子和多离子反应体系来提高电池的能量密度。基于这种原理，我们通过多变量协同效应，开拓电池材料的研究视野。我们的目标是实现电池能量密度和电动汽车行驶里程的飞跃。

My group proposed a light-element, multi-electron, and multi-ion reaction system to improve energy density of batteries. Based on this approach, we can coordinate different variables and expand the horizon for battery material research. Our goal is to achieve a leap in energy density of batteries and driving range of electric vehicles.

翟：杨教授研究的阻燃材料可用于社会保障和反恐措施的需求。

Flame-retardant materials studied by Prof. Yang could serve anti-terrorism and social security needs.

杨：我们开发了无卤的绿色阻燃材料，因为卤素是一族对健康和环境有不利影响的化学元素。我们团队首先采用了聚磷酸铵作为高效阻燃剂并且进行了规模化的生产制造。清洁技术、功能耦合和工业应用是我们所追求的新一代阻燃材料的三大要素。

Our research focuses on developing environmental friendly flame retardants without halogen, since halogens are a group of chemical elements that usually have adverse health and environmental effects. My group is the first one to use ammonium poly phosphates as high-efficiency flame retardants and to manufacture them. Clean technology, functional coupling, and industrial application are what we are seeking for the new generation flame retardant materials.

Naeem： 杨教授，请问阻燃材料的研究还有哪些内容？

Prof. Yang, could you tell us what else is involved in the reasearch on the flame retardant materials?

杨： 我希望扩大阻燃材料的跨学科探索。除了阻燃的功效，我们还利用纳米技术来实现其他更好的性能。同时，将聚合物化学与消防安全评估结合起来研究也很重要。

I also expect to expand the interdisciplinary study of these materials. In addition to improve the flame retardant capacity, we also need nanotechnology to achieve other preferred properties. It is important to integrate polymer chemistry with fire safety evaluation studies.

离开了吴教授和杨教授的实验室，翟老师和留学生们看见一位青年教授在楼道里正阔步走来，便上前打招呼：

Whey they leave Prof. Wu and Prof. yang's Laboratory, Prof. Zhai and students see a young professor striding along the corridor. Prof. Zhai steps forward to greet him.

翟: 张教授，您好。您手里拿着的有趣的图片是什么？
Hello, Prof. Zhang. What is the interesting picture in your hand?

纳米新能源材料
Novel Energy Nanomaterials

张教授把图片出示给大家观看。
Prof. Zhang shows the picture to everyone.

Attia: 这又是什么新材料？
What kind of new material is this?

张: 这是结合了纳米3D打印和超材料技术而发展出来的一类纳米新能源材料。利用原子尺度上的阳离子交换，来实现纳米晶的精准掺杂和金属纳米异质结的界面构建。这种方法从根本上

第二章　材以养德，料以治学

提高了等离子振荡激元中热电子注入半导体壳层的效率，使其量子产率达到48%。

This is a type of new energy nanomaterials with novel properties developed with the integration of nano 3D printing and super-material technologies. Atomic-level exchange technique was employed to achieve precise doping of nano crystals and hetero-interface on metals. The approach has radically improved the efficiency of plasmonic hot electron injection into the semiconductor shell, with a quantum yield of up to 48%.

Adnan: 这是怎么实现的？

How was this achieved?

张： 我们提出了一种全新的半导体纳米晶界工程的设计策略，通过精准掺杂与纳米界面化学的结合实现了纳米材料合成技术的升级。这一技术升级将会促进光电、光磁纳米材料、信息和能源电子技术的新发展。

My group proposed a novel semiconductor nanocrystalline grain boundary engineering (GBE) strategy. The nano materials synthesis methods were upgraded through the combination of precise doping and nano-interface chemistry. The technological upgrade will also lead to development of opto-electronic, opto-magnetic materials, information technologies, and electronic technologies.

Tahir: 张教授，请问这项技术的科学意义是什么？

What is the science prospect of this technology, Prof. Zhang?

张： 这种设计策略不仅揭示了半导体纳米结构电子

掺杂的内在机理，还为开发光学可切换的磁性纳米材料提供了线索。精确合成微纳米结构、精准掺杂、大规模的自组装，并结合3D打印技术是高效纳米功能器件的应用关键。

The approach reveals the mechanism underpinning electronic doping of semiconductor nano structures, shedding light on developing optically switchable magnetic nano materials. Precise synthesis of micro-nano-structures, large-scale assembly and 3D printing are the key to the development of nano energy materials with new properties, involving application of highly-efficient functional devices.

翟：谢谢张教授的讲解！
Thank you for your explanation, Prof. Zhang!

众人参观了五号楼实验室，又回到翟老师的办公室。
The crowd come back to Prof. Zhai's office again after visiting the laboratorys in No. 5 teaching building.

Emmanuel：翟教授，今天我们真是开阔了眼界，见识到很多高深的材料科学理论和技术前沿的研究进展，可是我们还是不知道选择什么样的研究课题，从哪儿入手去开展科研。
Prof. Zhai, today is an eye-opening day for us. We have been introduced to lots of advanced materials science theories and cutting-edge research progress. However, I still don't know what research topic to choose, and where to start about my own research.

翟：选择什么样的课题，首先是要了解这个阶段材

第二章　材以养德，料以治学

料科学的研究热点。其次，要对某个领域的课题有研究兴趣。再次，要和你们以前所学的知识结构衔接起来。我建议你们多去拜访材料学院的各位教授，深入了解他们的研究内容，来确定自己的导师，选择自己的博士论文课题。

Well, the principle to choose research topic is, first of all, to understand the research hot topics at present. Second, you should have curiosity and be interested in the topic. Last but not least, your research should connect with the structure of knowledge system that you have now. I suggest you should visit other professors in the school of MSE and get to know what they are doing to identify who should be your supervisor, and then choose a Ph. D. thesis topic.

Emmanuel：好的，谢谢翟教授。那么我们约时间改天再见，现在我们还要去学校的各个部门把在北理工的生活安排好。

All right. Thank you very much. We will go to other divisions in BIT to settle down our campus life. See you next time.

翟：祝你们顺利，改天再见。

Wish you good luck. See you next time.

材料学院 + 院徽

School of MSE + the School Badge

参考文献：

A Framework for Boosting Material Impact，*Nature*，vol. 567，No. 7748，2019.

重点词汇
Keywords & expressions

金属有机框架材料	metal-organic framework，MOF
久负盛名	renowned
高熵合金	high-entropy alloy，HEA
协同效应	synergistic effect
延展性	ductile
调幅	spinodal
强化相	strengthening phases
固溶体	solid solution
基体	matrix
耐腐蚀性	corrosion resistance
抗氧化性	oxidation resistance
非晶的	non-crystalline
能量密度	energy density
卤素	halogen
聚磷酸铵	ammonium polyphosphate
功能耦合	functional coupling
跨学科探索	interdisciplinary study
3D 打印	3D printing
超材料技术	super-material technology
阳离子	cation
掺杂	doping
界面	interface

| 等离子震荡激元 | plasmon |
| 晶界工程 | grain boundary engineering, GBE |

*阿卜杜勒·萨拉姆奖（Abdus Salam Award）已由故巴基斯坦物理学家、诺贝尔物理学奖得主阿卜杜勒·萨拉姆教授设立，由巴基斯坦科学院和发展中国家科学院授予，是巴基斯坦最负盛名的科学奖项，用以奖励不超过35周岁的青年科学家在化学、物理、数学、生物学等基础科学领域的研究。

Set up by Abdus Salam—a late Pakistani physicist and Nobel physics laureate, the Abdus Salam Award is the most well-known science award in Pakistan awarded to young scientists aged under 35 for their research in basic scientific areas such as chemistry, physics, mathematics and biology.

2.3 材料科学的研究课题
Research Topics in the School of MSE

2.3.1 功能有机高分子Ⅰ——聚集诱导发光材料
Functional Polymer Ⅰ—Aggregation Induced Emission

Souleymen：董教授，您好，很高兴见到您。

AIE

Hello, Prof. Dong. Glad to meet you.

董: 你好。

Nice to meet you.

Souleymen: 我是Rafei Souleymen，来自阿尔及利亚，想要在北京理工大学攻读博士学位。我听过您的大名，希望了解您的科研领域。

I am Rafei Souleymen from Algeria. I would like to pursue my Ph. D. in Beijing Institute of Technology. Could you introduce some backgrounds about your research?

董: 好呀，那我先问你一个问题。我们日常生活中有各种光电器件，比如：太阳能电池或者生物传感器。在这些器件中使用的有机染料是固态的还是液态的？

Well, let me ask you a question first. There are many opto electronic devices in our daily life, such as solar cells and bio sensors. Are the organic dyes in these devices in solid state or liquid state?

Souleymen: 呃，固态的吧，那样才更容易携带和使用。

Um, solid state, I think. It is more convenient to carry or use.

董: 对的。今天我就要给你介绍一个新的概念：聚集诱导发光，或者简称AIE。

Right. I would like to introduce a new concept to you today. That is, aggregation induced emission, or AIE for short.

Souleymen: 聚集诱导发光？这是什么意思？它和传统概

念有什么区别呢？

Aggregation induced emission? How is this concept different from traditional ones?

董： 发光材料是材料科学中重要的研究领域。我们知道，传统有机染料会在溶液中有很强的荧光发射。但是，当应用到固体薄膜或者在分子高浓度状态或者聚集状态时，荧光的发光强度就会被严重减弱直至完全湮灭。这种现象被称为聚集导致猝灭，简称ACQ。自从1954年福斯特教授发现了浓度猝灭效应，ACQ这个术语就被正式命名，迄今已有半个多世纪。可是，浓度猝灭效应的技术瓶颈极大地限制了传统有机发光材料的应用。

As we all know, fluorescence of organic dyes can be significantly weakened or annihilated at high concentrations or when in an aggregated state, which is aggregation-caused quenching, ACQ for short. ACQ has been documented for more than half a century since Förster's discovery of the concentration quenching effect in 1954.

Souleymen：我们日常许多染料都有这样地性质，我们都叫它们ACQ物质吗？

Many of the dyes used in our daily life have such properties, so are they all called ACQ substances?

董：是的，也可以叫它们ACQ发光团。
Yes, you can call them ACQ-gens, as well.

Souleyman：那什么是聚集诱导发光呢？
Then, what is aggregation induced emission?

董：大约在20年前，科学家们又合成了一些发光物质，却可以反其道而行之。当它们在孤立体系里或者溶液状态时，荧光很弱；而当其聚集时或者在固体薄膜中，则会有显著增强的、更有效的荧光发射。聚集诱导发光现象的出现成功地挑战了发光团的聚集不利于发光这一通识。
Some luminogenic materials were synthesized by scientists about 20 years ago. They act in a diametrically opposite way to what ACQ does. They emit very weak fluorescent light in isolated system or in solution, while emitting more efficiently when they aggregate or in the form of film. This is called aggregation induced emission (AIE). The emergence of AIE successfully challenges the common belief that gen aggregation is not conducive to luminescence emission.

Souleymen：太奇妙了！
Quite amazing!

董：是的。AIE材料体系的原创性研究打破了传统发光染料的"阿喀琉斯之踵"困境，将分子越聚集、材料发光越强变成了现实。AIE材料的研究由中国科学家主导,为新材料的研究开辟出了一片全新领域。

Yes. The original research of AIE is breaking the predicament of "the Achilles Heels" of traditional luminescent dyes. The more aggregated the gen molecules are, the more intense the fluorescence emission is. The research of AIE is dominated by Chinese scientists who have opened a whole new field for materials science.

Souleymen:神奇的AIE现象的机理是什么呢?是不是意味着在溶液中聚集诱导发光团必须要有可以自由运动的基团呢?

What is the mechanism of this magical AIE phenomenon? Does it mean that the AIE-gens need to have a part that can move freely in the solution state?

董:对极了。从理论分析和实验结果都一致揭示了AIE的内在机理是分子内运动受限,简称RIM。RIM包括分子内转动受限和分子内振动受限,两者共同作用于AIE效应。

Exactly. Experimental results and theoretical analysis have consistently revealed the fact of the restriction of intra-molecular motions, abbreviated for RIM. RIM includes the restriction of intramolecular rotations (RIR) and the restriction of intramolecular vibrations (RIV), both attributing to the mechanism of the AIE effect.

Souleymen:AIE效应真是一个神奇的发现。AIE染料能在哪些领域得到应用呢?

AIE phenomenon is really a magical discovery. Which fields can AIE dyes be applied to?

董: 感谢科研工作者们的辛勤工作，AIE分子在光电子器件制造、敏感环境检测和生物传感与成像等领域已经被开发应用，例如：制备高效有机发光二极管的发射器、生物影像探针等。

Thanks to the hard work of the researchers, AIE molecules have been applied in the fields of photoelectronic device, sensitive environment detection, biosensors and imaging. For example, they could be excellent emitters for the fabrication of efficient organic light-emitting diodes, biological imaging probes, and so on.

Souleymen: 太好了，我加入您的实验室就能掌握更多AIE发光分子团的应用技术了。

Wonderful! I want to know more specific applications about AIE-gens in the following days if I join in your lab. Thanks a lot!

董: AIE分子的发现和深入研究还获得了2017年度国家自然科学奖一等奖，我也荣幸参与到了其中。

The discovery and in-depth research of AIE won the First Prize of 2017 National Natural Science Award of China and I'm honored to be a part of it.

Souleymen: 恭喜您！我想把聚集诱导发光材料作为我博士

第二章 材以养德，料以治学

学位的研究方向。可以吗？

Congratulations! I would like to take AIE as my research direction for my Ph. D. thesis, can I?

董： 当然可以。这是一个开放的、值得继续深入的广阔领域，只有瞄准科学研究的前沿才能大有作为。

Of course you can. This is an open field that deserves further exploration. Only by aiming at the frontier of scientific research can you achieve higher goals.

Souleymen：那我从什么材料体系入手呢？

So from which material system should I start?

董： 现在有上千种AIE分子系统，你可以从多芳基吡咯体系和多芳基1,3-丁二烯体系这两类材料开始研究AIE现象，会更容易获得成果。

There are thousands of AIE molecule systems. You could start with multiaryl pyrrole(MAP) system and multiaryl 1,3-butadiene(MAB) system. It's easier to get results starting from these perspectives.

Souleymen：董教授，谢谢您花时间为我讲解，我现在明白多了。我马上去检索调研最新的研究进展和学术文献。

Thanks for your time, Prof. Dong. I understand this topic much better now. I will go to search for literature on the latest research progress immediately.

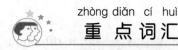

Keywords & expressions

功能有机高分子	functional polymer
聚集诱导发光	aggregation induced emission, AIE
阿尔及利亚	Algeria
荧光	fluorescence
聚集导致猝灭	aggregation-caused quenching, ACQ
发光团	gen
分子内运动受限	restriction intra-molecular motions, RIM
分子内转动受限	restriction of intramolecular rotations, RIR
分子内振动受限	restriction of intramolecular vibrations, RIV
发光二极管	light-emitting diode, LED
生物影像探针	bio logical imaging probe
多芳基吡咯	multiaryl pyrrole, MAP

2.3.2 功能有机高分子Ⅱ——阻燃材料
Functional Polymer Ⅱ—Flame Retardant Materials

Naeem 来到李教授的办公室。

Naeem comes to Prof. Li's office.

Naeem: 李教授，您好。我是来自巴基斯坦的留学生 Muhammad Naeem，我还取了一个中文名字叫雷佳翰。

第二章 材以养德，料以治学

Hello, Prof. Li. I am a Pakistani student. My name is Muhammad Naeem. I also have a Chinese name Lei Jiahan.

李：很好听的名字，很中国化，哈哈。

Ha-ha. Very nice name, typical Chinese one.

Naeem：李教授，我想在您的指导下攻读阻燃材料方向的博士学位！

Prof. Li, I wish to pursue the Ph. D. degree under your guidance in the area of flame retardant materials.

李：能先讲讲你学习这个方向的动机吗？

Tell me more about your motivation first, please?

Naeem：我听说阻燃材料是北京理工大学的特色学科，坊间都在流传"阻燃技术哪家强，北京理工找Prof. 杨"！

I hear that the flame retardant materials is one of the feature research areas in BIT, and it is widespread that "Where to find the best flame retardancy technology? Go find Professor Yang in Beijing Institute Technology!"

李：这就是业界的口碑。我们拥有国家级研究平台——国家阻燃材料工程技术研究中心，主任就是杨教授。你的选择非常正确！

We own the research platform at the national level, National Engineering Research Center for Flame Retardant Materials, and the director of the center is Professor Yang. You have made the wise choice!

Naeem：老师，什么是阻燃材料呢？

Professor, what are flame retardant materials?

李：你之前通过网络或者其他途径了解过吗？

Have you ever learned some information from the Internet?

Naeem：材料分为四大类，包括金属材料、无机非金属材料、高分子材料和复合材料，可是没有阻燃材料呀？

Materials are divided into four categories, including metal materials, inorganic non-metallic materials, polymer materials and composite materials. There is no flame retardant materials included.

李：阻燃材料一般是指阻燃高分子材料。由于高分子材料如塑料、橡胶和纤维等易于燃烧，会危害到公共安全，因此我们要对高分子材料进行阻燃处理，得到的产品就是阻燃材料啦！

Flame retardant materials generally refer to flame retardant polymer materials. As we know, polymer materials such as plastic, rubber and fiber are easy to burn, which will endanger public safety, so we need to carry out flame retardancy treatment on polymer materials. Thus the additives to improve the flame retardancy are named as flame retardant, and the final products with inflammability are flame retardant materials!

Naeem：阻燃材料都应用在哪些领域呢？

What are the applications of flame retardant materials?

李：石油化工、电子电器、建筑材料、交通运输、医疗卫生、生产制造等很多领域。日常

第二章 材以养德，料以治学

生活中的家电外壳、汽车内饰和外墙保温层中都能发现阻燃材料的影子。

In many other fields, for example, petrochemical, electronics and electrical appliances, construction materials, transportation, health care, production and manufacturing, and so on. In our daily life, flame retardant materials can be found in the shells of household appliances, car interior decoration, insulating layers of external walls, and so on.

Naeem：您能举一个阻燃材料应用的实例吗？

李：2019年的四月，注定是一个不寻常的四月。一场大火烧毁了法国的巴黎圣母院，这让无数善良的群众感到痛心。如果在巴黎圣母院的建筑材料中含有一定比例的阻燃材料，燃烧速度不会那么快，消防队员就来得及去灭火，烧蚀程度也不会那么严重，重建时也不会太困难。所以我希望在重建过程中，法国的建筑师们能考虑使用和添加我们的阻燃材料。

April 2019 was doomed to be an unusual month. A raging fire destroyed the Notre Dame in Paris, France, leaving countless people sad. If the construction materials of Notre Dame had contained a certain percentage of flame retardant materials, it would not have burnt that fast. Fire fighters would have had time to put out the fire, the burning would not have been that severe and it would not be too hard to rebuild. So I wish that French architects will consider using and adding our flame retardant materials during the reconstruction process.

Naeem: 您说的很有道理呀。
What you said is quite reasonable.

李: 雷，你可曾做过研究工作？
Naeem, have you ever engaged in any reseach wort?

Naeem: 我曾经为一位教授的铝合金项目做过研究助手。
I was a research assistant for a professor's project on alunimium alloy.

李: 不要紧。只要有决心和行动力，你学起来没问题。
Never mind. You will catch on quickly with determination and the ability to execute.

Naeem: 我在您的课题组将会学习到哪些专业知识和技能呢？
What knowledge and skills will I learn in your research group?

李: 阻燃剂的合成制备、功能高分子的加工、材料结构的表征和性能的测试等实验技能，以及科研论文的绘图写作技能。
Experimental skills such as synthesis and preparation of flame retardant materials, processing of polymer materials, characterization of structure and testing of properties and performance for materials, as well as scientific drawing and writing skills for scientific research papers.

第二章 材以养德，料以治学

Naeem：毕业后我能选择什么职业呢？

What about my career choice after graduation?

李：可以去研究机构或企业继续从事阻燃材料的研究、开发及相关工作。

You can join a research institute or enterprise to continue the research and development of flame retardant materials or choose related job.

重点词汇
Keywords & expressions

阻燃材料	flame retardant materials
无机非金属材料	inorganic non-metallic materials
塑料	plastic
橡胶	rubber
纤维	fiber
巴黎圣母院	Notre Dame in Paris

2.3.3 功能有机高分子Ⅲ——生物医用材料
Functional Polymer Ⅲ—Biomedical Materials

Attia 来到了冯教授的研究室。

Attia comes into Prof. Feng's laboratory

Attia：您好，我是Attia，您一定是冯教授。

Hello, I'm Attia. You must be Prof. Feng.

冯: 是的。很高兴见到你，Attia。请坐。

Yes, I am. Good to see you, Attia. Take a seat, Please.

Attia: 冯教授，我希望了解您的科研内容。您能给我介绍一下吗？

Prof. Feng, I hope to know more about your research. Could you give me a brief introduction?

冯: 可以。我们实验室主要从事的是生物医用材料与超分子聚合物的研究，特别是在血管组织工程中采用可降解聚酯进行功能化修饰。

Fine. My group's research mainly focuses on biomedical materials and super-molecular polymers, especially the functional modification of degradable polyester in biomedical materials on vascular tissue engineering.

Attia: 感谢您，大健康是当今时代的一个重要的主题。将材料和生物学结合，非常有意思。那什么是生物医用材料？什么又是血管组织工程呢？

Thank you. Massive Health is an important theme of the age. It is very attractive to combine materials science and biology in related research. So, what are biomedical materials? And what is vascular tissue engineering?

冯: 生物医用材料是用来对生物体进行诊断、治疗、修复或替换病损组织、器官的材料。血管

第二章 材以养德，料以治学

组织工程是指利用细胞和生物可降解材料来制备、重建和再生人工血管替代物。我们致力于对可降解聚酯进行功能化修饰来制备血管组织工程材料，属于第三代生物材料的范畴。

Biomedical materials are materials used to diagnose, cure, repair or replace damaged tissues, organs, or enhance its function. Vascular tissue engineering utilizes normal cells and biodegradable materials of vascular wall to fabricate, reconstruct and regenerate artificial vascular substitutes. Currently, we are devoted to functional modification on biodegradable polyester for vascular tissue engineering, which belongs to the third generation of bio-materials.

Attia: 第三代生物医用材料主要特点是什么？

What are the main features of the third generation of bio-materials?

冯: 第三代生物医用材料的特点是能在分子水平上刺激细胞，产生特殊应答反应的生物材料。可降解材料能够在降解过程中为细胞的增殖和功能化提供很好的空间，有助于组织的再生。

The third-generation of bio-materials are characterized by the study of biological materials that stimulate cells to produce specific responses at the molecular level. Degradable materials provide a good space for cell proliferation and functionalization during degradation and contribute to tissue regeneration.

Attia: 采用可降解聚酯的功能化修饰有什么作用呢？

What is the significance of functional modification of biodegradable polyester?

冯: 对可降解聚酯的修饰可以提高其生物相容性，并使得其可以更好地调控细胞的增殖和生长，降低生物毒性，促进组织的再生。

The functional modification can improve the bio-compatibility of the biodegradable polyester so that they can better modulate cells' growth and proliferation to reduce biological toxicity, and promote tissue regeneration.

Attia: 您能再讲解一下怎么实现可降解聚酯的功能化修饰吗？

Could you explain more on functional modification?

冯: 可降解聚酯的功能化修饰，主要是采用功能性分子、氨基酸、多肽、蛋白质进行接枝改性，以使得材料在生物体内实现良好的功能性。

The major strategy is grafting functional molecules including amino acid, peptide and protein into the polyester. These functional molecules will play important roles in improving the in vivo functional behaviors of bio-materials.

Attia: 您是怎么制作这种具有功能性的人工血管的呢？

How do you manufacture the functional artificial blood vessels?

冯: 我们主要通过电纺丝技术来制备人工血管。

第二章 材以养德，料以治学

还有一些其他的方法，例如：端基肝素化、表面肝素化和表面涂布含肝素的水凝胶等来制备可降解聚己内酯人工血管移植物。当然，人工血管的制备技术正在不断地革新和进步中，比如时尚的3D打印方式，也可以实现人工血管的制造。

We mainly use electro-spinning method to fabricate artificial blood vessels. There are also other methods, such as end group heparinization, surface heparinization and surface coating of heparin-containing hydrogels to prepare degradable polycaprolactone artificial blood vessel grafts. Manufacturing technology of artificial blood vessels is continuously upgraded and improved. For instance, 3D printing is also used to fabricate artificial blood vessels nowadays.

Attia：感谢您的指导，我对生物医药材料，特别是您说的人工血管有了深刻的理解，这也给我的研究提供了一个很好的思路。

Thank you for your instruction. I have a deeper understanding of biomedical materials, especially the artificial blood vessels you mentioned. This will also enlighten my own research.

冯：人工血管，特别是小口径人工血管是世界性的难题，远期的通畅率和钙化是难以克服的困难，需要更多的研究人员投入到这个领域中。

The research on artificial blood vessels, especially artificial blood vessels with small diameters, is a global challenge. To maintain long-term patency rate and avoid calcification is formidably difficult. It requires more and more intelligent researchers to be committed to this field.

Attia: xiè xiè féng jiào shòu wǒ yuàn yì cóng shì zhè xiàng yán jiū lái jìn lì jiǎn
谢谢冯教授！我愿意从事这项研究来尽力减
qīng bìng rén de tòng kǔ
轻病人的痛苦。

Thank you, Prof. Feng. I will definitely carry out the research to alleviate the suffering of patients as soon as possible.

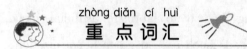

Keywords & expressions

生物医用材料	biomedical materials
超分子聚合物	supr-molecular polymer
可降解的	degradable
聚酯	polyester
血管组织工程	vascular tissue engineering
功能化修饰	functional modification
诊断	diagnosis
增殖	proliferation
生物相容性	bio-compatibility
生物毒性	biological toxicity
氨基酸	amino acid
多肽	polypeptide
蛋白质	protein
电纺丝	electro-spinning
肝素化	heparinization
钙化	calcification

2.3.4 功能有机高分子Ⅳ——天然高分子材料
Functional Polymer Ⅳ—Natural Polymer Materials

Tahir 来到陈教授的办公室。
Tahir comes to Prof. Chen's office.

Tahir：陈教授，您好。您的研究方向是什么？
Hello, Prof. Chen. Could you tell me about your research direction?

陈：我们组主要对天然高分子材料进行研究。
My group is mainly engaged in the research on natural polymer materials.

Tahir：天然高分子材料的研究对象有哪些？
What are the research targets of natural polymer materials?

陈：按照原料分类的话，研究对象以天然高分子及其改性物为主，比如，壳聚糖，羧甲基壳聚糖，海藻酸钠和抗性淀粉等。按照产物种类分类的话，研究对象可以分为水凝胶，气凝胶，微球，海绵等。
According to the classification of raw materials, the research objects are mainly natural polymers and their derivatives, such as chitosan, carboxymethyl chitosan, sodium alginate and resistant starch. According to the classification of products, the research subjects can be divided into hydrogels, aerogels, microspheres, sponges and so on.

Tahir: 您的课题组研究些什么内容呢？

What are the highlights of the research of your goup?

陈: 我的课题组研究在保证生物相容性的同时，通过多种方式提高或赋予天然高分子水凝胶其他新颖的、有用的性质，如抗菌性，pH响应性，电场响应性等。

My group aims to improve the properties or to confer natural polymer hydrogels new properties, such as antibacterial property, pH responsiveness and electric field responsiveness, while ensuring their biocompatibility.

Tahir: 天然高分子水凝胶用途有哪些？

What about the applications of natural polymer hydrogels?

陈: 我的课题组制备的天然高分子水凝胶可以用于止血材料，药物释放，超级电容器等。其中，天然高分子抗菌止血材料在2018年第四届中国"互联网+"大学生创新创业大赛中获得全国赛银奖，并作为创业项目入驻北京理工大学科技园进行孵化。

The natural polymer hydrogels prepared by my group can be used for hemostatic materials, drug release, super capacitors and so on. And the project of antibacterial hemostatic natural hydrogels won the National Silver Award in the 4th China College Students "Internet Plus" Innovation and Entrepreneurship Competition in 2018, which was the base of a startup at the Science and Technology Park of BIT for incubation as an entrepreneurial project.

Tahir: 请问陈教授，博士在读期间的研究内容如何确定？
Prof. Chen, how should I decide the research topic during doctoral study?

陈: 博士在读期间的研究内容可与导师商议确定。除了研究课题以外，在读期间还可以选择参与课题组内部的多种活动，如创业大赛等。
The research topic during the doctoral period can be chosen after consultation with the supervisor. Apart from research topics, students can also choose to participate in various activities of our research group, such as entrepreneurship competition.

Tahir: 您对申请人的硕士专业或本科专业有限制吗？
Are there any restrictions on the majors of applicants?

陈: 我对申请人硕士或本科的专业没有限制，欢迎具有不同教育背景的同学前来报名。
I set no restrictions on the applicant's major of master degree or bachelor degree. Students with different educational backgrounds are all welcome to apply for a position at my research group.

Tahir: 谢谢陈教授！
Thank you, Prof. Chen.

重点词汇
Keywords & expressions

天然高分子材料	natural polymer materials
壳聚糖	chitosan
海藻酸钠	sodium alginate
淀粉	starch
水凝胶	hydrogel
气凝胶	aerogel
海绵	sponge
抗菌的	antibacterial
止血材料	hemostatic materials
药物释放	drug release
创业大赛	entrepreneurship competition

2.3.5 电子封装技术
Electronic Packaging Technology

Adnan 来到了电子封装技术专业赵教授的办公室。

Adnan comes to the office of Professor Zhao whose research field is electronic packaging.

Adnan：赵教授，您好，感谢您的接待。听说电子封装技术是材料学院的一个新专业，是这样吗？

第二章 材以养德，料以治学

Hello, Professor Zhao. Thank you for your time. I heard that the electronic packaging technology is a relatively new research direction in the School of MSE. Is this true?

赵：是的。电子封装技术专业是2007年由教育部批准，在国内两所高校率先进行试点建设的。它是北京理工大学十大特色专业之一，也是经教育部批准的"卓越工程师教育培养计划"的专业之一。

Yes. The electronic packaging technology is relatively new compared with other educational programs though it has already become one of top-ten featured majors in BIT. In 2007, the electronic packaging technology program was approved by the ministry of education, and BIT was one of the first two universities in China who established this major in that year. In addition, the electronic packaging technology program is also among the excellent engineer education and training programs granted by the Ministry of Education.

Adnan：感谢您简要介绍了专业历史。我有几个关于电子封装技术的问题想请教您。首先，请问您"封装"指什么？

Thank you for the briefing on history of this program. Now, I would like to ask some questions regarding the electronic packaging technology. First of all, could you please explain what the term "packaging" exactly means?

赵：很好的问题。半导体元器件的出现，改写了电子工程的历史。但是，你知道，半导体元器件

· 113 ·

既不能以裸露的形式单独、可靠地工作，在没有物理集成之前，也不能作为一个系统一起来工作。于是，"封装"的概念就出现了。

That is a very good question. The advent of semiconductor device has reshaped the history of electrical and electronics engineering. However, the semiconductor devices cannot work alone in the form of bare components, nor can it work together as a system without physical integration. This is how the concept of "packaging" comes into being.

Adnan： "封装"概念的起源非常有意思！那电子封装技术又是什么？

A very interesting origin of the "packaging" notion! Then, what exactly is electronic packaging technology?

赵： 从广义上说，任何有助于电子元件物理集成的技术都可以视为电子封装技术。从狭义上说，电子封装是将单个电子元件互连成为单个微系统的制造技术，从而确保微系统在设定的工作环境中有效地运行。

In the broad sense, any technology contributing to the physical integration of the electronics components can be regarded as the electronic packaging technology. In the narrow sense, the electronic packaging is the manufacturing technology to interconnect individual electronics components into a single micro-system, thereby ensuring the effective and efficient performance of the micro-system in its designated working environment.

第二章 材以养德,料以治学

Adnan: 下一个问题是,电子封装技术包含哪些类型的工艺技术?

Next, I would like to know about the types of technologies included in the electronic packaging.

赵: 一般说来,常用的电子封装技术包括电子封装和电子组装。举几个例子,比如有:双列直插式封装、球栅阵列式封装和更为现代的扇出型晶圆级封装等。

Typically, the common electronic packaging technology includes the electronic packaging process and the electronics assembly process. To name a few, for example, the dual in-line packaging(DIP), the ball grid arrays(BGA) packaging, and more modernly, the fan-out wafer-level packaging(FO - WLP), and so on.

Adnan: 我还需要学习理解更多的专业术语。那么,电子封装的主要作用是什么呢?

Well, I still need to learn many more terminologies. What are the main functions of the electronic packaging?

赵: 主要有五个作用:电源分配、信号分配、散热通道、机械支撑和环境保护。

The main functions of the electronic packaging can be categorized into five aspects, namely, electrical power distribution, electrical signal interconnection, thermal management, mechanical support, and environmental protection.

Adnan: 电子封装技术中具体封装的是什么元器

What kinds of individual components are involved in the electronic packaging then?

赵: 封装也分为不同的级别。零级封装是集成和封装芯片本身；一级封装是互连其他分立的电子元器件，如电容、电感和芯片；二级和三级封装分别组装电子板卡和母版。

The electronic packaging can be graded into different packaging levels. Traditionally, the packaging level-zero integrates and packages the chip itself. Packaging level-one interconnects other discrete electronic components, such as capacitors and inductors with the chip. Packaging level-two and level-three assembly the individual electrical broad and motherboard, respectively.

Adnan: 那不同的级别的封装是否对应不同的技术呢？

Does it mean that each different packaging level has its own corresponding packaging technology?

赵: 当然。例如一级封装主要包括引线键合、倒装芯片等；二级封装主要是通孔安装、表面安装。

Absolutely. For instance, packaging level-one mainly involves wire-bonding technology, flip-chip technology and so on. Packaging level-two includes through-hole assembly technology and surface mounting technology (SMT).

Adnan: 赵教授，您能给简单地描述一下封装的大致

第二章 材以养德，料以治学

流程是怎么样的吗？

Next, Professor Zhao, could you please briefly describe a typical electronic packaging process for me?

赵：好的。在集成电路芯片中，典型的电子封装工艺包括了晶圆镶边、晶圆划片、芯元黏合、线键合、复合成型和切边等工序。

Certainly. The typical electronic packaging process for an integrated circuits (IC) chip would involve wafer taping, wafer dicing, die-attachment, wire bonding, compound molding, and trimming.

Adnan：电子封装工艺在科研中的常用设备有什么？

What are the most commonly-used facilities and equipment for the research of electronic packaging process?

赵：我们在研究中配备了许多专业仪器设备，包含全自动贴片机、BGA/CSP 精密表贴芯片返修设备、通孔器件返修仪、薄膜沉积设备、印刷线路板制板设备、光刻机、纳米粉末冶金和烧结设备、可焊性测试仪、剪切强度测试仪、多功能引线键合设备、三维共焦光学显微镜、三维高分辨电子显微镜、薄膜应力应变分析系统以及多种微尺度分析设备和可靠性测试设备。

At present, we have been equipped with numerous specialized instruments in those facilities, including automatic die-attachment instrument, BGA/CSP precision surface-mounting instrument, through-hole device repairing instrument, thin-film deposition instrument, printed circuit board manufacturing instrument, photolithography instrument, nano-scale powder metallurgy and sintering instrument, solderability tester, shear strength tester, multiple function wire-bonder, 3D confocal optical microscope, 3D high-resolution electron microscope, thin film stress/strain analyzing system, micro-scale experimental analysis facility, multiple reliability testing equipment, and so on.

Adnan: 哇，有这么多设备可用于科研呀。听上去这个专业有很好的就业前景，那电子封装技术未来的发展趋势是什么呢？

Wow! That is a lot of equipment available for the research. Sounds very interesting to me. I have learned that this major has a very promising career path after graduation. I was wondering what would be the future development trend in the field of electronic packaging technology.

赵： 由于电子器件的总体发展趋势是小型化、多功能、数据高速传输，所以电子封装技术的发展将在电子工程这些趋势中扮演决定性的角色。

The general trend of the electronics components and engineering is towards miniaturization, multiple-functionalization, and high-speed data transportation. Accordingly, the development of the electronic packaging technology would play a determining role in the trends of the advancement of the electronics engineering.

Adnan：您回答了我所有的疑问。今天我学到了许多电子封装的知识。感谢您详尽的介绍！

Well, you have answered all of my questions. Today, I have learned a lot of knowledge about electronic packaging technology. Thank you very much for the detailed introduction!

赵：不客气。我代表我们专业的老师，鼓励、欢迎优秀的外籍留学生来电子封装专业攻读博士学位。

It is my pleasure. On behalf of our faculty members, I encourage and welcome our talented international students to study for doctoral degree in the major of electronic packaging technology.

 重点词汇

Keywords & expressions

电子封装技术	electronic packaging technology
封装	packaging
组装	assembly
双列直插式封装	dual in-line packaging, DIP
球栅阵列式	ball grid arrays, BGA
扇出型晶圆级封装	fan-out wafer-level packaging, FO－WLP
晶圆	wafer
电容	capacitor
电感	inductor
芯片	chip
芯元	die

集成电路	integrated circuit, IC
应力	stress
应变	strain
失效分析	failure analysis
成型	molding
切边	trimming
沉积	deposition
光刻	photolithography
粉末冶金	powder metallurgy
微尺度	micro-scale
烧结	sintering

2.3.6 新能源材料与器件
New Energy Materials and Devices

Emmanuel 来到了位于五号楼九层的环境科学与工程北京市重点实验室，他见到了苏教授。

Emmanuel drops in on Prof. Su when he comes to Beijing Key Laboratory of Environmental Science and Engineering on the ninth floor of No. 5 Teaching Building.

Emmanuel：苏教授，您好。我对能量存储和能量转化材料感兴趣，您能给我讲一讲吗？

Hello, Prof. Su. Could you tell me something about energy storage and conversion materials? I am very interested in them.

第二章　材以养德，料以治学

苏： 能量转化和存储有几种主要的器件：燃料电池、太阳能电池和二次电池等。

There are several main devices for energy conversion and storage, namely, fuel cell, solar cell, secondary battery, and so on.

Emmanuel： 您能分别介绍一下这几种新能源器件吗？

Could you please introduce these new energy devices respectively?

苏： 燃料电池是把燃料的化学能直接转化为电能并且输出的器件。太阳能电池本质上是一个大面积半导体二极管，它利用光伏效应把光能，尤其是太阳光能转换成电能。而把电能转换后，以化学能形式存储起来，可以反复使用的器件就是我们通常说的可充电电池，又称为二次电池。二次电池放电后，可以通过再次充电将电极材料激活，又能继续存储电能。二次电池可反复充放电数千次，所以更加经济实用。这几种新能源器件的核心就是要开发新能源材料，我们学院有不少教授正在研究。

Fuel cell is a device that converts the chemical energy of a fuel directly into electrical energy and outputs it. Solar cell is essentially a large-area semiconductor diode, which utilizes the photovoltaic effect to convert light energy, especially solar light energy, into electrical energy. The device that converts the electric energy and stores it in the form of chemical energy is what we usually call the rechargeable battery, also known as secondary battery. When a secondary battery is discharged, the electrode material can be activated again by recharging and then the electric energy is stored again. The secondary battery can be discharged and charged thousands of times, so it is more economical and practical. The core of these new energy devices is to explore new energy materials. Quite a few professors in the school of MSE are doing research on it.

Emmanuel: 苏教授，您能多谈谈二次电池的研究内容吗？
Prof. Su, could you talk a little more about the research of secondary batteries?

苏: 现在二次电池领域的绝对主角是锂离子电池。1980年，西班牙科学家Michel Armand首先提出"摇椅式电池"的概念后，美国科学家Goodenough合成出钴酸锂作为锂离子电池的第一个可靠的正极材料，揭开了锂离子电池快速发展的序幕。2019年10月，Goodenough和其他两位科学家因为在锂离子电池研究中的卓越贡献而共同获得了诺贝尔化学奖。

Lithium-ion battery (LIB) now is the absolute leading role in the secondary battery field. The Spanish scientist Michel Armand proposed the "rocking chair battery" mechanism for the lithium ion rechargeable battery in 1980. Soon, the US scientist John B Goodenough's research started the prelude to the rapid development of LIB by adopting lithium cobalt oxide ($LiCoO_2$) as the first reliable positive electrode material for LIBs. In October, 2019, Goodenough and two other scientists won the Nobel Prize in Chemistry for their outstanding contributions to the research of lithium-ion batteries.

Emmanuel：太棒了！什么是"摇椅式电池"？这个概念太奇妙了。

Brilliant! What is the "rock chair battery" mechanism? The concept is magical.

苏：摇椅式电池机理指的是在二次电池中用嵌锂化合物代替纯金属锂作为电极材料。在充放电过程中，锂离子处于从正极到负极又回到正极的运动状态，像在摇椅的两端来回奔跑，提高了电池的循环性能和储存容量。

The "rock chair battery" mechanism refers to using Li based intercalation compound to replace pure metal lithium as electrode materials in the secondary battery. During the charging and discharging process, lithium ions are in motion from positive electrode to negative electrode during charge stage and back to positive electrode during discharge process, like running back and forth between the ends of a rocking chair, improving the cycle performance and storage capacity of the battery.

Emmanuel：锂离子电池研究有哪些值得研究的内容？

What are the worth-studying research contents of lithium-ion batteries?

苏：锂离子电池可分为四个部分：阳极、阴极、电解液和隔膜。每个部分的材料都是当前重要的研究内容。

Lithium-ion batteries can be divided into four parts: anode, cathode, electrolyte and separator. The materials system of each part is an important research content nowadays.

Emmanuel：锂离子电池现在可真"火"呀。

Research on lithium-ion batteries is hot right now.

苏：在当今快速移动的世界里离不开充电电池，笔记本电脑、摄影录像设备、智能手机这些现代文明的产物无不依赖和渴求高质量的充电电池。纯电动汽车不仅可以减少燃油汽车的尾气排放，净化大都市的空气质量，同时也是时尚的标准。除了特斯拉汽车，中国的汽车制造厂家也不断推出各种新型电动汽车。2018年，各类锂离子电池的销售产量超过100亿颗。

We can't do much without rechargeable batteries in today's fast-paced world. Such products of modern civilization as laptops, video cameras and smartphones, all rely on and desire for high-quality rechargeable batteries. Pure electric vehicles not only reduce exhaust emissions from oil-powered vehicles and clean up the air quality of metropolises, but also stand for a fashionable standard. In addition to Tesla cars, Chinese automakers are rolling out new electric vehicles. Sales of various kinds of lithium-ion batteries have exceeded 10 billion units in 2018.

第二章 材以养德，料以治学

Emmanuel： 超越锂离子电池，下一代二次电池还有哪些呢？

What is the next generation secondary battery beyond lithium ion battery?

苏： 下一代二次电池研究还包括锂离子电池系列的锂硫电池、锂空气电池，碱金属离子电池系列的钠离子电池、钾离子电池，以及多价态金属离子电池系列的镁离子电池、铝离子电池等。研究目标是进一步提升电池的能量和功率密度、降低制造成本、增加循环次数，保障使用安全。最近，退役锂离子电池的回收利用也引起人们的关注。

The next generation secondary battery includes LIBs series, such as lithium sulfur battery and lithium air battery; alkali metal ion battery series, such as sodium ion battery and potassium ion battery; polyvalent metal ion battery series, such as magnesium ion battery and aluminum ion battery. The research goal is to further improve energy and power density, reduce manufacture cost, increase cycle times and ensure the safety. The recycling of spent batteries has also raised great concerns recently.

Emmanuel： 苏教授，您能设想一下终极可充放的能量存储器件是什么样的吗？

Prof. Su, could you imagine what the ultimate form of the rechargeable energy storage device would be like?

苏: 你看过《变形金刚》吗?
Have you ever seen the movie *Transformers*?

Emmanuel: 嗯,很好看的电影,我喜欢机智、热情的大黄蜂。
Yeah, fantastic movie, and I like the smart and enthusiastic Bumblebee.

苏: 哈哈。我说的是,你注意到汽车人和飞机人所争夺的能量块了吗?它具有极高能量密度,即插即用,携带和使用方便。能量块的载体就是我们心目中的终极可充放的能量存储器件。
Well, my point is the energon in the movie that Autobots and Decepticons fought for. Do you get it? It possess an extremely high energy density, and is easy to carry and use. The carrier of the energon is the ultimate form of rechargeable energy storage device in my mind.

Emmanuel: 我明白了!为了能量块而努力!
I see. Let's work to create the energon!

重点词汇

Keywords & expressions

新能源材料与器件	new energy materials and devices
能量存储	energy storage
能量转化	energy conversion

燃料电池	fuel cell
太阳能电池	solar cell
电池	battery
光伏效应	photovoltaic effect
锂	lithium，Li
离子	ion
摇椅式电池	rocking chair battery
钴酸锂	lithium cobalt oxide，$LiCoO_2$
诺贝尔奖	Nobel Prize
正极	positive electrode
负极	negative electrode
容量	capacity
阳极	anode
阴极	cathode
电解液	electrolyte
隔膜	separator
尾气排放	exhaust emission
硫	sulfur，S
碱金属	alkali metal
钠	sodium，Na
钾	potassium，K
镁	magnesium，Mg
铝	aluminum，Al

2.3.7 低维功能纳米材料
Low-dimensional Functional Nanomaterials

在参观了各个材料实验室后，Naveed来到低维功能纳米材料实验室曹教授的办公室。

After visiting various materials laboratories, Naveed comes to Prof. Cao's office in the Low-dimensional Functional Nanomaterials Laboratory.

Naveed： 曹教授，您好。久仰您的大名，您的声望在巴基斯坦留学生中有口皆碑。

Hello, Prof. Cao. I have heard of you for many times. Your reputation is well known among the Pakistani students.

曹： 谢谢。我在2004年冬天第一次来到了巴基斯坦，参加了第二届布尔班应用科学技术国际会议。我很快就喜欢上了这个美丽的国家和这里淳朴的人民。到了2007年，有一名巴基斯坦留学生瓦赫德和我联系，希望来我的实验室学习纳米技术，我就满口答应了他，瓦赫德成为我的第一名外籍研究生。从那时起，每年都有外籍留学生来到我们实验室开展科研工作，攻读博士学位。迄今为止，已有不少于15名外籍学生获得了博士学位，

第二章 材以养德，料以治学

大多数都来自巴基斯坦。

Thank you. I first came to Pakistan in the winter of 2004 to attend the 2nd International Bhurban Conference on Applied Science and Technology (IBCAST). I soon fell in love with this beautiful country and its honest people. When a Pakistani student Waheed wrote to me that he wished to learn nanotechnology in my lab in 2007, I promised him without hesitation. So, Waheed became my first international student. From then on, international students come to my group and carry out scientific research every year. So far, at least fifteen international students have got doctoral degree in my laboratory. Most of them come from Pakistan.

Naveed： 感谢您对巴基斯坦留学生的教导和培养！曹教授，我有一些问题向您请教。首先，低维功能纳米材料中的"低维"是什么意思？

Thank you so much for your instruction and cultivation for Pakistani international students. Prof. Cao, I have some questions. The first is what "low-dimension" means in low-dimensional functional nanomaterials?

曹： "维度"指的是材料结构上的空间尺度。低维纳米材料包括零维的量子点，一维的纳米管、纳米棒、纳米线，二维的纳米片和薄膜等尺度上小于100纳米的材料。

"Dimension" refers to the spatial scale of material structure. Low-dimensional nanopmaterials include zero-dimensional quantum dots, one-dimensional nanotubes, nanorods, nanowires, two-dimensional nanosheets and thin films with the size of depth smaller than 100

Naveed： 尺度在纳米级别的材料和常规材料有什么不同呢？

What is the difference between nano scale materials and conventional materials?

曹： 纳米材料常常具有一些特殊的物理化学性质，如：量子尺寸效应、表面效应，隧穿效应等。当材料的晶粒尺寸下降到某一个很小的纳米尺度，金属微粒费米能级附近的电子能级将由准连续变为离散，半导体微粒出现能带隙展宽，这就是量子尺寸效应。纳米材料的表面原子数目增多，表面能增大，化学活性急剧增强，这是表面效应。纳米微粒的外层电子还具有轻易穿越势垒的能力，称为隧穿效应，这会导致微电子领域和芯片行业摩尔定律的最终失效。

Nanomaterials often have some special physical and chemical properties, such as quantum size effect, surface effect and tunneling effect. With the grain size of a metal particle decreases to nanoscale, the electron levels in the energy band near the Fermi level will change from quasi-continuous to discrete, while the band gap of the semiconductor nanoparticle would be widened. This is the so-called quantum size effect. The number of surface atoms increases when the size of grain decreases to nanoscale, the surface energy increases and the chemical activity increases sharply, which is the surface effect. The outer shell electrons of nanoparticle also have the ability to cross the energy band barrier easily which is known as the tunneling effect. This could lead to the eventual failure of Moore's Law in microelectronics and chips.

Naveed: 怎样才能合成出纳米材料和纳米结构呢？
How can we synthesize nano materials and nano structures?

曹: 总体来说有两种途径，就是"自底而上"的方法和"由顶向下"的方法。"自底而上"的方法是在最底层自主操控一个个原子，是通过组装实现预期的结构和性能。而"由顶向下"的方法，是通过物理或化学的方法把大尺寸的块体材料变小，直到成为纳米颗粒，比如机械粉碎、球磨、剥离或化学合成等技术。"明星材料"石墨烯最初就是通过机械剥离法获得的。

In general, there are two approaches, that is, bottom-up and top-down. The bottom-up approach is to self-manipulate atoms from the lowest ground through assembly to achieve the desired structure and performance. The top-down approach means to reduce the size of large blocks of materials to nano particles by physical or chemical techniques, such as mechanical grinding, ball milling, stripping, and chemical synthesis. The star material, graphene, was originally obtained by mechanical exfoliation.

Naveed: 那么，低维功能纳米材料里面的"功能"体现在什么地方？

Then, what does the "function" mean in low-dimensional functional nanomaterials?

曹："功能"指的是开发新材料的除机械性能之外，优良的电学、光学、磁学等性能。我的课题组的主要科研方向是，开发出化学能和电能之间高效转化的可再生的清洁绿色能源新材料，降低化石燃料使用过程中的二氧化碳排放量。这也是现代文明社会的科研主题之一。

"Function" means to develop new materials with excellent electrical and optical properties. The main research direction of our laboratory is to develop renewable clean green new energy materials which have efficient mutual conversion between chemical energy and electrical energy, reducing the dependence on fossil fuels. This is also one of the scientific research themes of modern civilized society.

Naveed：您能详细介绍一下吗？

Could you give me some details?

曹：我来讲两个例子。氢气是质量能量密度很高的清洁能源，电解水生产氢气和氧气的反应是最基础的化学反应。然而，工业电解水的效率却很低。如何高效、便捷地用电解水和光电解水制氢是重要的研究内容。目前使用的铂金属催化剂非常昂贵,它在中国俗称"白金",可见它的稀缺性。通过深入研究水电解过程中两个基元反应:析氢反应和析氧反应,我们合成了低维纳米电催化材料。它具有高的电化学比表面积和电荷传输速率,表现出很低的过电位,高效地促进了水解制氢的反应效率。

Let me give you two specific examples. Hydrogen is a well-known clean energy with high mass energy density. The electrolysis of water to produce hydrogen and oxygen is the most basic chemical reaction, yet subject to a low efficiency at industrial application. Producing hydrogen by water electrolysis or photoelectrolysis efficiently and conveniently is of great significance. The widely used metal Platinum catalysts are very expensive, and commonly known as "white gold" in China due to its scarcity. My group have synthesized a low-dimensional electrocatalyst in nanoscale through studying two elementary reactions in the process of hydroelectrolysis, that is hydrogen evolution reaction (HER) and oxygen evolution reaction (OER). The electrocatalyst has high electrochemical specific surface area, high charge transfer rate and very low overpotential, and improves the electrolytic water reaction with high efficiency.

曹: 另外一个例子是,我们利用生物仿生的特性,采用米糠、生物质玉米、蚕丝这些天然作物原材料合成出多种爆米花类型衍生的多孔碳材料和多功能碳基纳米片材料。将这种材料用于超级电容器中,能极大地提高器件的储能容量——比常规的石墨材料高5倍以上,经过10 000次的充放电循环后,它的容量衰减很小,不超过10%。而且,这种合成方法制备工艺简单,容易放大规模生产。

Another example. We synthesize various porous carbon materials and functional carbon-based nanosheets by biomimetics method using natural biomass crops including rice bran, corn, and silk as precursors for application in supercapacitor. These porous carbon materials can exhibit the specific capacity five times than that of graphite counterpart and significantly improve the overall capacity of the supercapacitor devices. Furthermore, these porous carbon materials can show excellent cycling stability with no more than 10% capacity fading over 10,000 cycles. This synthesis technology is simple and scalable.

Naveed: 曹教授,请问什么是超级电容器?超级在哪儿?

What are supercapacitors and what is super performance?

曹: 超级电容器是一种新型能量存储器件。相比于传统电容器,它的静电存储容量要大三个数量级以上,也就是大了几千倍,甚至上万倍。这就是它的超级之处。

Supercapacitors are a new type of energy storage device, which has more than three orders of magnitude larger, which means thousands of times or even tens of thousands of times larger electrostatic storage

第二章 材以养德，料以治学

capacity than traditional capacitors.

Naveed： 超级电容器为什么会有这么神奇的功效呢？
Why do supercapacitors have such amazing performance?

曹： 超级电容器的神奇之处，在于它的内在储电机理分为双电层电容和法拉第赝电容。我们将合成的低维纳米功能材料制成活性电极，通过在活性电极的表面层及表面附近发生可逆的氧化还原反应来实现化学能和电能的存储与转换，产生法拉第赝电容，使它具有类似于二次电池的储能特性。
The intrinsic mechanism of supercapacitors consists of double layer capacitors and Faraday pseudo-capacitors. Using as-synthesized low-dimensional functional materials make the active electrode of supercapacitors, and the chemical energy was stored and converted by the reversible redox reaction on and near the surface of the active electrode. Thus the Faraday pseudo-capacitors were generated, which is similar to the energy storage characteristics of secondary batteries.

Naveed： 太奇妙了！可是，曹教授，要获得博士文凭好艰苦呀！我的汉语交流能力又差，能有什么捷径吗？
Fantastic! However, Prof. Cao, it's so hard to get the Ph. D! And my Chinese communication ability is not good. Is there any shortcut to take?

曹： 你既然不远千里来到中国，就不应当满足于在这里混个文凭，不能把语言问题当作学不好的借口。只要选好课题方向，耐下心来，一定会做出拿得出手的科研成果来。

Since you came to China from thousands of miles away, you shouldn't dawdle away your time and just get a diploma here. Language problem isn't an excuse. As long as the right research direction is determined, keep patient and persistent. You will certainly achieve pretty good and fruitful scientific research outcomes.

Naveed：真是百闻不如一见！曹教授，我对您心悦诚服，可以请您做我的导师，指导我在材料学专业的科研工作吗？

Seeing is believing. I'm quite convinced of you. Hope you could be my supervisor to instruct my research in MSE major.

曹：好呀，欢迎加入低维功能纳米材料实验室。

All right. Welcome to low-dimensional functional nanomaterials laboratory.

曹教授和他的巴基斯坦留学生们
Prof. Cao with his Pakistani students

经过和材料学院各位教授的接触和双向选择，Emmanuel 和其他的外籍留学生都找到了自己的学术导师和满意的研究方向。

After visiting professors in the School of MSE and the two-way selection, these international students have all confirmed their own academic supervisors and satisfactory research directions.

重点词汇

Keywords & expressions

低维功能纳米材料	low-dimensional functional nanomaterials
纳米管	nanotube
纳米片	nanosheet
量子尺寸效应	quantum size effect
表面效应	surface effect
隧穿效应	tunneling effect
费米能级	Fermi level
离散	discrete
能带	energy band
势垒	energy band barrier
摩尔定律	Moore's Law
由顶向下	top down
自底而上	bottom up
球磨	ball milling
石墨烯	graphene
机械剥离	mechanical exfoliation
化石燃料	fossil fuel

二氧化碳	carbon dioxide
氢	hydrogen,H
氧	oxygen,O
电解水	water electrolysis
铂	platinum,Pt
催化	catalysis
基元反应	elementary reaction
析氢反应	hydrogen evolution reaction,HER
析氧反应	oxygen evolution reaction,OER
比表面积	specific surface area
过电位	overpotential
超级电容器	supercapacitor
生物仿生	biomimetics
石墨	graphite
衍生	derivative
电极	electrode
法拉第赝电容	Faraday pseudo-capacitance
氧化还原反应	redox reaction

第三章 学有所成不负韶华
Succeed in Research, Paying off the Youth

3.1 材料实验室生存法则
Survive at Materials Laboratory

培养安全意识

实验室安全须知

Emmanuel 准备进入实验室开展科研实验，他向翟教授提出申请，请求得到允许。

Emmanuel is ready to enter the laboratory to carry out his scientific experiments. He asks Prof. Zhai for permission.

翟：Emmanuel，你需要经过学院的实验室安全培训，才可以正式进入实验室。

Emmanuel, you need to go through the school's laboratory safety training before you are officially allowed to enter into the laboratory.

Emmanuel：您能先给我讲一讲，实验室安全最主要的几点注意事项吗？

Could you give some details in advance about the most important rules for laboratory safety?

翟： 没问题。在实验室里要有强烈的安全意识，良好的安全行为习惯和有效的安全管理，使安全得到保障。

Certainly. The priority of entering into a laboratory is a strong sense of safety, reflected by good safety behavior habits and effective safety management rules.

Emmanuel： 为什么要有强烈的安全意识？

Why should we hold the strong sense of safety?

翟： 如果在实验室里出现了事故，后果会很严重。所有人的安全都是一个整体，别人的安全也是你的安全。因此，不要问警钟为谁而鸣——它就是为你而鸣。

If there is an accident in the laboratory, the consequences can be extremely serious. We are all on the same boat to guarantee laboratory safety, and the safety of others is the safety of yours. Therefore, don't ask for whom the alarm tolls—it bells for you.

Emmanuel： 培养良好的安全行为习惯，需要注意哪些方面？

What should I pay attention to in the good safety behavior habits?

翟： 进入实验室，有四样装备必不可少：工作服、胶皮手套、口罩和护目镜，用来保护好自己的人

shēn ān quán
身安全。

In order to protect your personal safety, before entering the laboratory, four indispensable pieces of equipment are needed—laboratory coat, rubber gloves, respirator and goggles.

zuò shí yàn qián yào hé zhǐ dǎo lǎo shī tǎo lùn yī xià nǐ de shí yàn fāng àn shì
做实验前要和指导老师讨论一下你的实验方案是
fǒu ān quán kě kào　yào dé dào lǎo shī yǔn xǔ cái kě yǐ jìn xíng
否安全可靠，要得到老师允许才可以进行。

Discussing with your supervisor whether your experimental plan is compulsory before carrying out the experiment. You cannot do it without the permission of the teacher.

shǐ yòng měi ge yào pǐn qián　yào rèn zhēn de liǎo jiě tā de xìng zhì　　lì
使用每个药品前，要认真地了解它的性质。例
rú　tā shì fǒu yì rán yì bào　shì fǒu yǒu dú　tā de zhù cún tiáo jiàn shì
如：它是否易燃易爆？是否有毒？它的贮存条件是
shén me　fáng hù cuò shī yòu shì shén me　rán hòu　yán gé àn zhào yāo qiú
什么？防护措施又是什么？然后，严格按照要求
hé guī fàn lái shǐ yòng yào pǐn
和规范来使用药品。

You need to be clear about the nature of each chemicals before using it. For example, whether it is flammable or explosive, whether it is toxic, what its storage conditions are, and what its protective measures are. Then you may use the chemicals in strict accordance with the requirements.

shǐ yòng yǒu huī fā xìng　qì wèi nóng liè de yào pǐn shí　yào zài tōng fēng
使用有挥发性、气味浓烈的药品时，要在通风
chú lǐ jìn xíng shí yàn　tóng shí jiàng dī tōng fēng chú de bō lí mén
橱里进行实验，同时降低通风橱的玻璃门。

When using a volatile, strong-scented drug, you need to do it in a fume hood and lower its glass door.

shǐ yòng qì píng qì tǐ shí　yí dìng yào gé wài xiǎo xīn jǐn shèn　suǒ yǒu qì
使用气瓶气体时，一定要格外小心谨慎。所有气
píng dōu yào fàng zhì zài fáng dǎo jià zhōng　shǐ yòng qián yào jiǎn chá qì píng
瓶都要放置在防倒架中，使用前要检查气瓶

的气密性,气路要连接良好。使用管式炉通气时也要保证整个装置系统的气密性良好。使用后要关紧气阀。

Be careful when using the gas in the gas cylinder. All cylinders should position in anti-falling racks. Check the air tightness of the cylinder before using; gas paths should be well connected. When gas is used in the tube furnace, you should ensure that the air tightness of the device system is good. Close the gas valve after using it.

使用加热装置时,要保证加热装置电路连接良好、控温装置良好,防止反应中出现爆破、喷液等危险现象。

When you use the heating device, it is necessary to ensure the electrical circuit with the apparatus is well connected and the temperature control device is good to prevent dangerous incidents such as blasting and spraying.

当你第一次使用先前没有用过的仪器时,首先要向老师或同学请教它的正确操作方法和注意事项。不要擅自盲目开启,否则有可能会损坏仪器,并且造成事故。

Ask the teacher or lab mates for the correct manipulation and precaution rules when you want to operate the apparatus that you have not used before. Do not operate it randomly; otherwise the apparatus may be damaged.

Emmanuel: 知道了,我一定会严格遵守实验规范。

I understand. I will strictly abide by the experimental rules.

Emmanuel：那么，有效的实验室管理要求我们做到什么？

Then, what is the effective safety management?

翟：实验过后要在第一时间进行归置整理。打扫实验台面，清洁实验仪器，检查仪器电路是否完全关闭。用过的药品要放回原位，实验过程中产生的废液不能随意排放，要分类放置。

Sort out all the apparatus after doing the experiment at once. Clean the lab bench, clean the experimental instrument, turn off the power source completely, and put back the used medicine. Classify the waste liquid generated during the experiment and place them in a fix position. You must not drain off the liquid at random.

❖ 废弃化学品处理

Disposal of Waste Chemicals

废弃化学品

Emmanuel：实验室的废旧试剂要怎么处理？

How shall I deal with the waste liquid and the waste reagents in the laboratory?

翟：将它们分类放置，在网上申请报废。由学校资实处每周集中回收处理。

Classify and place them separately, and apply for discarding process online. The Office of National Asset and Laboratory Management at

BIT will collect information and deal with the applications every week.

Emmanuel：还有哪些实验室管理的措施呢？
Then, what is effective safety management?

翟：要及时回收废弃实验物品；定期打扫实验室，保持整洁干净；每天晚上最后离开的同学要全面检查，关闭水、电、气路，拍照上传工作群，再关灯、关门，才能离开。
Recovery of discarded experimental items must be done properly. Clean the whole laboratory thoroughly and regularly, keeping everything clean and tidy. Every night the last one who leaves should shut down the water, electricity and gas faucets, and take photos, uploading them to the work group, and then turn off the lights and close the door before leaving.

Emmanuel：什么时候进行实验室大扫除？
How often is the laboratory cleaning done?

翟：根据学院要求，我们要定期进行实验室的内部整改，每周五下午三点开始打扫。
According to the requirements of the school, we have to carry out laboratory internal inspection regularly. The cleaning work is usually done at 3 p.m. every Friday.

Emmanuel：好的，我有哪些具体的工作职责？
All right. What are my assigned duties?

翟：你主要负责清理仪器及擦拭表面灰尘。Naveed 负责收集清理废旧物品，比如：不用的包装纸箱和泡沫，损坏的玻璃仪器以及生活垃圾等。

You are mainly responsible for cleaning the instrument and dusting their surface. Naveed is responsible for collecting and discarding the waste, such as unused cartons and foam, damaged glassware and household garbage.

Emmanuel：没问题。

No problem!

翟：还有一些其他的详细规则，比如危险品标示、事故紧急处理方法等，你可以通过实验室安全培训或者上网查阅相关文件来学习。

There are also some other detailed rules for dangerous goods labeling, emergency handling methods, and so on. You can learn them through the laboratory safety training or reading the relevant documents online.

Emmanuel：好的。

Okay.

翟：Emmanuel，要时刻记住：实验万千类，安全第一位，操作不规范，亲人两行泪。

Emmanuel, always remind yourself: experiments are countless, but safety is the priority; unregulated manipulations lead to tragedies or our beloved ones' tears.

Emmanuel：我记住了。等我通过了实验室安全培训，我就可以自信地行走在五号楼里啦！

I'll keep that in mind. When I have passed the laboratory safety training, I will be able to stride across No. 5 Teaching Building!

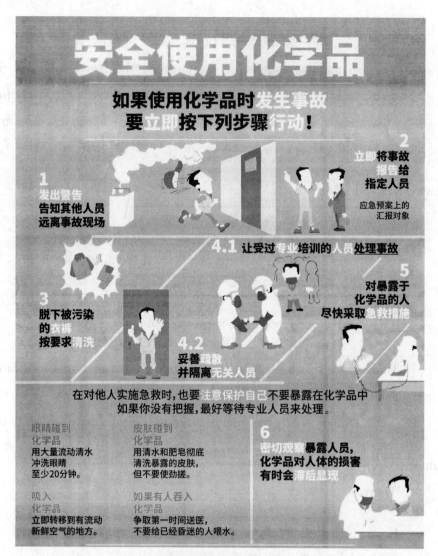

huà xué pǐn shì gù chǔ lǐ
化 学 品 事 故 处 理
Chemicals Accident Treatment

重点词汇

Keywords & expressions

安全培训	safety training
安全意识	safety awareness

事故	accident
工作服	laboratory coat, work clothes
胶皮手套	rubber gloves
口罩	respirator, mask
护目镜	goggles
化学品	chemicals
易燃的	flammable
易爆的	explosive
有毒的	toxic
挥发性	volatile
通风橱	fume hood
气瓶	gas cylinder
防倒架	anti-falling rack
气密性	air tightness
管式炉	tube furnace
气阀	gas valve
爆破	blasting
喷液	spraying
废液	waste liquid
危险品标示	dangerous goods labeling
玻璃仪器	glassware

3.2 实验室的工作和生活
Work and Life at Laboratory

实验室安全制度

Emmanuel 已经进入实验室开展实验了，在实验室的工作学习生活中他与同学们相处得很愉快。

Emmanuel has already entered the laboratory to carry out the experiments and has been getting along well with his classmates.

刘：Emmanuel，课题组决定从下周一开始执行考勤制度，要求周一至周五每天早上八点、下午两点按时到达实验室，不允许迟到。

Emmanuel, the group has decided to implement the attendance checking system from next Monday, requiring that we arrive at the laboratory on time at 8 am and 2 pm every day from Monday to Friday. Late arrivals are not allowed.

Emmanuel：有时我有急事不能到的话，应该怎样处理呢？

What should I do if I sometimes can't make it due to emergency?

刘：有事不能到的时候，提前在微信工作群里请假，写明原因。

When you can't get there, ask for leave in the WeChat work group in advance and specify the reason.

Emmanuel：好的，我会严格遵守的。

Okay, I will strictly obey it.

刘：另外，本学期的卫生值日表已经安排好了，张贴在门右边的墙上，记得要按时值日。

In addition, the sanitary duty schedule for this semester has been arranged. It has been posted on the wall to the right side of the door. Remember to be on time when you are on duty please.

Emmanuel：刘钰，你好。你有时间吗？我需要你的帮忙。

第三章 学有所成 不负韶华

Hello, Liu Yu. Do you have time? I need your help.

刘: 什么事情？

What's up?

Emmanuel: 我需要买一些实验用品。

I need to buy some experimental supplies.

刘: 你需要先填写一份你需要买的用品清单，拿去给老师签字，然后找王国庆同学帮你下单。

You need to fill in a list of supplies you need to buy and take it to the teacher for signature, and then ask Wang Guoqing to place the order for you.

Emmanuel: 你知道哪里有空白的用品清单吗？

Do you know where the blank list of supplies is?

刘: 我这里有一份电子版，你拿去打印一份吧。

I have an electronic version here. You can print it out.

Emmanuel: 我打印好了，你能帮我填写一下吗？

I have printed it. Can you help me to fill it out?

刘: 嗯，你说一下你想要买什么吧。

Well, tell me what you want to buy.

Emmanuel: 我需要买一个圆底烧瓶，两个烧杯。

I need to buy a round bottom flask and two beakers.

刘: 你需要说清楚它们的规格。

You need to clarify their sizes.

Emmanuel: 圆底烧瓶要500mL的，烧杯要一个100mL，一个

250mL 的。

The capacity of the model of round bottom flask is 500mL; the capacity of one beaker is 100mL and the other is 250mL.

刘：除了这些，你还要购买一套个人专用的实验服，手套和口罩。

Besides, you also need to buy a set of personal laboratory suits, gloves and masks.

Emmanuel：没有到货以前，我该怎么办？

What should I do before the supplies arrive?

刘：321实验室的门后有一些备用的实验服，你可以暂时穿一件。

There are some free lab coats behind the door of Lab 321. You can wear one temporarily.

Emmanuel：手套和口罩，每样都买一盒，可以吗？

Can I buy one box of gloves and one box of masks?

刘：可以。购物清单填好了，你拿去给老师签字吧。

Sure! The shopping list is filled out; you can take it to the teacher for permission.

Emmanuel：谢谢！

Thanks!

Emmanuel：对了，你知道303实验室的钥匙在哪里吗？303实验室的门没有开，我需要进去做实验。

Before I forget, do you know where the key to Lab 303 is? The door of Lab 303 is closed, and I need to go in and do experiments.

第三章　学有所成不负韶华

刘：我帮你找一下。在这儿，在王国庆同学的桌子上。
Let me find it for you. Oh here, on Wang Guoqing's desk.

Emmanuel：好的，我先去开门，用完后再把钥匙还回来。
Okay, let me open the door first, and return the key after using it.

刘：我跟你一起过去吧，我也有实验要做。
I will go with you. I also have experiments to do.

Emmanuel：正好我不会使用离心机，你能教我一下吗？
I don't know how to use the centrifuge. Can you teach me?

刘：可以。使用离心机的时候，样品要对称放入，转子要对称，保持重量平衡。可以用电子天平给样品称重。
OK. When using the centrifuge, you must put the sample into the rotor, which should be symmetrically balanced. You can use the electronic balance to weigh the sample first.

Emmanuel：之后呢？
And then?

刘：然后，在面板上设置时间和转速就可以了。
Then set the time and speed on the panel.

Emmanuel：好的，谢谢你。我想要离心清洗样品。
Okay, thank you. I want to use the centrifuge to clean the sample.

刘：清洗样品的时候，你可以用超声来使样品分散均匀。超声波清洗机在那边，使用的时候注

· 151 ·

意它的水位线要符合标准。

When cleaning the sample, you can use ultrasound to make the sample evenly dispersed. The ultrasonic cleaner is over there. When using it, make sure that its water level meets the standard.

Emmanuel：嗯，你知道哪里有离心管吗？我找不到了。

Well, do you know where the centrifuge tubes are? I can't find them.

刘：在实验室通风橱下面的柜子里。

Inside the cabinet under the fume hood.

❖ 接打开水

Getting Hot Water

如何接热水

Emmanuel：刘钰，请问哪儿可以接热水喝？

Liu Yu, could you tell me where I can get some hot water?

刘：你也像我们中国人一样喜欢喝热水了吗？

Well, do you get used to drinking hot water as we Chinese?

Emmanuel：入乡随俗嘛。

Yeah. When in China, do as Chinese do.

刘：你可以在楼里的自动热水机上接水。要提醒你，热水机里接出水的温度比较高，在接水的时候要小心，不要让水烫到自己。

You can get hot water from the automatic water electric heater in the building. Reminding you, be careful to get hot water. Don't burn yourself since the temperature of hot water and vapor is very high.

Emmanuel：谢谢提醒。不过，哪里有自动热水机？

Thank you for kindly reminding. However, where is the automatic water electric heater?

刘：自动热水机在每一层楼道尽头的热水间里。你将校园卡插入机器卡槽，就可以接到热水了。

The water heater is in the water booth at the end of every floor. When you insert the campus card in the slot of machine, you can get the hot water.

Emmanuel：我今天忘记随身带校园卡了……

I forgot to bring my campus card with me...

刘：没关系。实验室值日同学的一项职责就是每天用暖水瓶接满热水。你去倒热水喝吧。

Never mind. One of the responsibilities of students on duty in the lab is to fill thermos bottles with boiling water every day. You will go and get some hot water.

Emmanuel：太感谢了！

So many thanks!

刘：好说，很高兴能帮上忙。

Any time, I'm glad to help.

王：Emmanuel，在你正式进入课题研究前，我要指导你做几个经典的化学合成实验，来检验和训练你的实验技能。

Emmanuel, before you formally enter the research project, I want to

· 153 ·

guide you to do a few classic chemistry experiments to test and train your experimental skills.

Emmanuel：好的。我准备好了。

OK. I'm ready.

王：第一个实验是聚乙烯醇的缩醛化实验。去准备实验要用的仪器吧。

The first experiment is the acetalization experiment of polyvinyl alcohol (PVA). Go to prepare the equipment for the experiment first.

Emmanuel：我准备好了250毫升的三口烧瓶、球形冷凝管、机械搅拌器和水银温度计。

I have prepared a 250mL three-necked flask, a spherical condenser, a mechanical stirrer and a mercury thermometer.

王：你需要把它们组装起来。将三口烧瓶放入油浴加热装置中，将机械搅拌器插入三口烧瓶中，另外两个口分别连接温度计和球形冷凝管。

You need to assemble them. Put the three-necked flask into the oil bath heating device and insert the mechanical stirrer into a 250mL three-necked flask, with the other two ports of the three-necked flask connected to the thermometer and the spherical condenser.

Emmanuel：我组装好了。

I have assembled it.

王：在三口烧瓶中加入15克的聚乙烯醇，也就是PVA，再加入150毫升去离子水。打开搅拌设置，升温到90℃，让PVA完全溶解。

Add 150 mL of deionized water and 15 grams of polyvinyl alcohol into the 250 mL three-necked flask. Turn on the stirring setting, and raise the temperature to 90℃ to completely dissolve the PVA.

Emmanuel：好的，温度已经到90℃了，PVA已经完全溶解了。

OK, the temperature has reached 90℃, and the PVA has been completely dissolved.

王：现在加入3毫升的甲醛。搅拌15分钟之后，滴加浓度为1∶4的盐酸溶液，控制反应体系的酸碱度范围，也就是pH值在1到2之间，保持反应温度为90℃。

Now add 3 mL of formaldehyde and stir for 15 minutes, and then add a 1∶4 hydrochloric acid solution dropwise to control the pH range (pH value) of the reaction system at 1–2 and keep the reaction temperature at 90℃.

Emmanuel：怎样确定反应体系的pH值呢？

How to determine the pH value of the reaction system?

王：这里有pH试纸，你可以滴加反应液在试纸上，试纸会发生颜色变化，不同颜色对应不同的pH值，比对pH标准卡片可以确定数值大小。

Here is a piece of pH test paper. You can drop the reaction solution on the test paper. The color of the test paper will change. Different colors correspond to different pH values. The pH value is judged according to the color.

Emmanuel: 好的。
OK.

王: 继续搅拌，反应体系会逐渐变稠。当反应体系出现气泡或有絮状物产生时，立即加入8%的NaOH溶液，调节pH值为8~9，冷却处理。
Continue stirring, and the reaction liquid will gradually be thickened. When bubbles or flocs appear in the reaction system, immediately add 8% of NaOH solution, adjust the pH value to 8 – 9, and cool it down.

Emmanuel: 得到的无色黏稠液体就是聚乙烯醇缩甲醛吗？
Is the colorless viscous liquid the polyvinyl formal?

王: 是呀。这也是胶水的主要成分。
Yes. This is also the main ingredient of glue.

Emmanuel: 哦，知道了。
Oh, got it.

王: 今天，我们来做第二个实验，醋酸乙烯酯的乳液聚合反应。
Today, we will do the second experiment, the emulsion polymerization of vinyl acetate.

Emmanuel: 这个实验看起来很复杂呀。
This experiment looks very complicated.

王: 没关系，我们可以一起来完成。乳液聚合是以水为分散介质，单体在乳化剂的作用下分散，并且使用水溶性的引发剂引发单体聚合的方法。所生成的聚合物以微细的粒子状分散在水中,形成乳液。

It doesn't matter. We can do it together. Emulsion polymerization is a method in which water is used as a dispersion medium. With this method, monomers are dispersed under the action of emulsifiers, and water-soluble initiators are used to initiate monomer polymerization. The polymer produced is dispersed in water in the form of fine particles to form an emulsion.

Emmanuel: 我先搭建实验仪器,将它们组装好。将一个四口烧瓶放入油浴加热装置中,四个口分别连接滴液漏斗、温度计、搅拌器和回流冷凝管。

Let me first set up the experimental instruments and assemble them. Put a four-necked flask into the oil bath heating device, and connect the four ports to the dropping funnel, thermometer, stirrer and reflux condenser.

王: 我去称量需要的实验试剂。将90毫升去离子水加入到四口烧瓶中。这是称量好的5克聚乙烯醇,也加入烧瓶中。开启搅拌设置,将温度加热至90℃,使聚乙烯醇溶解。你再去准备两个小烧瓶吧。

I'll weigh the experimental reagents which I need. Add 90 mL of deionized water to the four-neck flask. This is 5 grams of polyvinyl alcohol to be added to the flask. Turn on the stirring setting and heat the temperature to 90℃ to dissolve the polyvinyl alcohol. Go ahead and prepare two small flasks.

Emmanuel：好的，拿来了。
Okay, here you are.

王：一个加入1克OP-10，一个加入1克过硫酸铵，分别用5毫升水溶解。
Add 1 gram of OP-10 to one flask, and add 1 gram of ammonium persulfate to the other, and dissolve them with 5 mL of water.

Emmanuel：我现在将溶液降温至60~65℃，然后停止搅拌，加入1克十二烷基磺酸钠，再重新开启搅拌。
I now cool the solution to 60 – 65℃, then stop stirring. Add 1 gram of sodium dodecyl sulfonate, and restart the stirring.

王：这是配置好的5毫升OP-10水溶液，加入到反应液中，再加入20毫升醋酸乙烯酯，混合均匀后加入配置好的2.5毫升的过硫酸铵溶液，开始反应。聚合反应开始后，我们要将溶液温度控制在68~70℃，最高不超过80℃的范围内。
This is the prepared 5 mL OP-10 aqueous solution. Add it to the reaction solution, and then add 20 mL of vinyl acetate. Mix them well and add 2.5 mL of the prepared ammonium persulfate solution to start the reaction. After the polymerization reaction starts, we need to control the temperature of the solution at 68 – 70℃, and the maximum should not exceed 80℃.

Emmanuel：已经过去30分钟了，我觉得种子乳液已经形成了。我们将剩余的2.5毫升的过硫酸铵溶液也加入吧。

Thirty minutes have passed, and I think the seed emulsion has formed. Let's add the remaining 2.5mL ammonium persulfate solution.

王：用滴液漏斗缓慢滴加剩余的醋酸乙烯酯，需要在两个小时内加完。

Use the dropping funnel to slowly add the remaining vinyl acetate dropwise, which needs to be completed within two hours.

Emmanuel：现在我们滴加完了。

Now we are done.

王：现在需要将溶液温度升至85℃，继续搅拌，保温反应30分钟后撤除恒温浴槽。

Raise the temperature to 85℃ and continue to stir. Keep the temperature for 30 minutes and remove the thermostatic bath.

Emmanuel：我去称量0.26克碳酸氢钠，用5毫升水溶解。温度现在是多少？

I will weigh 0.26 gram of sodium bicarbonate and dissolve it with 5 mL of water. What is the temperature now?

王：快到50摄氏度了。

It's almost 50℃.

Emmanuel：那我们把碳酸氢钠溶液加进去吧。另外再加5毫升的邻苯二甲酸二丁酯，充分搅拌使其混合均匀。

Let's add the sodium bicarbonate solution. In addition, add 5 mL of o-benzene dibutyl phthalate and stir well to make it evenly mixed.

王： 好啦，我们可以出料了。这就是市场上俗称的"白乳胶"。

Okay, we can get out the material; this is what is commonly called "white latex" in the market.

Emmanuel： 怎么能测试这次样品的固体含量？

How can I test the solid content of this sample?

王： 先称量空白培养皿的重量，记录为 m_0；倒入一些乳液，记录量量为 m_1；将它们放入烘箱中，完全干燥后，再来称量干燥后的重量，记录为 m_2；那么固体含量可以通过公式 $wt\% = (m_2 - m_0)/(m_1 - m_0)$ 计算获得。

Weigh the blank petri dish and record it as m_0. Pour some emulsion, and record the weight as m_1. Put them in the oven, and after a few hours, you weigh the dried weight and record it as m_2. Then the solid content can be calculated by the formula $wt\% = (m_2 - m_0)/(m_1 - m_0)$.

王： 我们做最后一个训练性实验：合成双金属层状氢氧化物。

We will do the last training experiment now: the synthesis of layered double hydroxides.

Emmanuel：这次没有现成的实验操作指导呀。

There is no ready-made experimental operation guide this time.

王：这次实验是以氧化亚铜为模板制备具有三维结构的双金属层状氢氧化物材料。

This experiment used cuprous oxide as a template to prepare the layered double hydroxides material with a three-dimensional structure.

Emmanuel：氧化亚铜模板怎么合成呢？

How shall we synthesize the cuprous oxide template?

王：氧化亚铜的制备采用化学沉淀法制备。称取4毫摩尔二水氯化铜，充分溶解在去离子水中。放于磁力搅拌器上，常温搅拌10分钟，得到无色透明的氯化铜水溶液。

The preparation of cuprous oxide adopts a chemical precipitation method. Weigh 4 millimoles of copper chloride dihydrate and dissolve it in deionized water. Put it on a magnetic stirrer and stir at room temperature for 10 minutes to obtain a colorless and transparent copper chloride aqueous solution.

Emmanuel：稍等一下，我拿本子记录下来。

Wait a moment, please. I will take a notebook and write it down.

王：好的。之后称取0.08毫摩尔的氢氧化钠，充分溶解在去离子水中。超声3分钟，使它分散均匀。然后将氢氧化钠溶液缓慢滴加到氯化铜水溶液中，常温搅拌30分钟，就会得到淡蓝色的氢氧化铜悬浊液。

OK! Then weigh 0.08 mmol of sodium hydroxide and fully dissolve it in deionized water. Use an ultrasonic machine to sonicate for 3 minutes to make it evenly dispersed. Then slowly add the sodium hydroxide solution dropwise to the copper chloride aqueous solution and stir at room temperature for 30 minutes to obtain a light blue copper hydroxide suspension.

Emmanuel：好的，我都记下了，然后呢？

Okay, I note it down. And then?

王：然后称取0.024毫摩尔的抗坏血酸，在水溶液中超声溶解，得到浓度为0.6mol/L的无色透明溶液。将抗坏血酸水溶液缓慢滴加到氢氧化铜悬浊液中并搅拌1小时，保持溶液温度为55℃。这时可以观察到悬浊液的颜色由蓝色逐渐变为绿色，再变为黄色。最后得到颜色变为橙红色的氧化亚铜悬浊液。

Then weigh out 0.024 millimoles of ascorbic acid and dissolve it in an aqueous solution ultrasonically to obtain a colorless and transparent solution with a concentration of 0.6 mol/L. Slowly add the fully dissolved ascorbic acid aqueous solution dropwise to the copper hydroxide suspension and stir it for 1 hour, keeping the temperature at 55℃. At this time, it can be observed that the color of the suspension gradually changes from blue to green, and then to yellow. Finally, it turns into an orange-red cuprous oxide suspension.

Emmanuel: 有好多颜色变化啊。
There are so many color changes.

王: 是的。将反应结束的悬浊液静置3小时。将静置后的氧化亚铜悬浊液再进行过滤操作,就得到氧化亚铜沉淀,随后进行离心冲洗操作。
Yes. After the reaction, allow the resulting suspension to stand for 3 hours, and filter the cuprous oxide suspension after the standing to obtain cuprous oxide precipitate, and then use the centrifuge to wash it.

Emmanuel: 怎样进行离心冲洗呢?
How to perform centrifugal washing?

王: 用水和乙醇分别离心冲洗三次,清洗掉杂质。离心机的转速设定为每秒500转,每次离心时长为2分钟。然后将氧化亚铜沉淀真空干燥8小时,最终得到干燥、纯净的样品。
Centrifuge and rinse them three times with water and ethanol. Set the rotation speed of the centrifuge to 500 rpm, and set the time of each centrifugation to 2 minutes to obtain a pure cuprous oxide precipitate. Then vacuum dry the cuprous oxide precipitate for 8 hours, and finally a dry and pure sample will be obtained.

Emmanuel: 真空干燥箱的温度设定为多少度呢?
What is the temperature setting of the vacuum drying oven?

王: 设定的干燥温度为60℃。所制备的氧化亚铜样品是三维立方结构,单个立方晶体的结构尺寸在几十到几百纳米之间。

Set the drying temperature at 60 ℃. The prepared cuprous oxide sample has a three-dimensional cubic structure, and the size of a single cubic crystal is between tens to hundreds of nanometers.

Emmanuel:那你能再带领我做一下后面的双金属层状氢氧化物的制备吗?

Can you instruct me with the preparation of the layered double hydroxides?

王:好的。双金属层状氢氧化物的制备同样采用溶液共沉淀法,即在溶液中使用化学试剂对氧化亚铜进行液相刻蚀,使溶液中的氢氧根离子与金属离子结合生成双金属层状氢氧化物。实验步骤是,首先称量50毫克氧化亚铜粉末,溶解在去离子水中,超声分散5分钟使之均匀;然后将氯化镍、氯化铁加入到氧化亚铜水溶液中,并且在磁力搅拌器上充分搅拌。

OK. The preparation of layered double hydroxides also adopts the solution co-precipitation method, in which chemical reagents are used to etch cuprous oxide, so that the hydroxide ions in the solution combine with metal ions to form bimetal layered hydrogen Oxide. First, weigh 50 micrograms of cuprous oxide powder, dissolve it in deionized water, and disperse it ultrasonically for 5 minutes to make it uniformed. Then add nickel chloride and ferric chloride to the cuprous oxide aqueous solution, and stir thoroughly with a magnetic stirrer.

Emmanuel: 要加多少氯化镍、氯化铁呢?

How much nickel chloride and ferric chloride should be added?

王: 保证铁元素和镍元素,即溶液中金属阳离子的总物质的量为0.25毫摩尔就好。配置浓度为1摩尔每升的硫代硫酸钠水溶液,取10毫升滴加到原混合溶液中,借助磁力搅拌器常温搅拌1小时,进行氧化亚铜的刻蚀,使其生成以氧化亚铜为框架的具有三维结构的镍铁金属层状氢氧化物。

Ensure that the total amount of iron and nickel or the total amount of metal cations in the solution is 0.25 millimoles. Prepare a sodium thiosulfate aqueous solution with a concentration of 1 mol/L, and add 10 mL dropwise to the original mixed solution. Stir for 1 hour at room temperature with a magnetic stirrer, and etch the cuprous oxide to generate the nickel-iron metal layered hydroxides with a three-dimensional structure with cuprous oxide as a framework.

Emmanuel: 这样就制备好了吗?

Is that done?

王: 还没有。我们观察到随着反应的进行,溶液体系的颜色由橙黄色逐渐转变成淡黄色。

反应结束后，静置悬浊液，抽滤将悬浊液静置1小时，随后离心冲洗，再干燥收集。

Not yet. We will observe that as the reaction progresses, the color of the solution system gradually changes from orange to light yellow. After the reaction, the suspension will stand for 1 hour, followed by centrifugal washing operation, and then dried and collected.

Emmanuel：这个环节的实验步骤怎么操作呢？

How is this part operated?

王：与之前的氧化亚铜的操作是一样的。至此，我们就完成了所有的制备过程。

The operation is the same as that of the previous cuprous oxide. At this point, we have completed all the preparation processes.

Emmanuel：得到这样的材料，有什么用呢？

What's the use of such materials?

王：我们会在后续的实验中测试它的电催化性能，以及它在电解水制氢气反应中的催化效率。

We will test its electrocatalytic performance and its catalytic efficiency in the reaction of electrolysis of waler to produce hyolrogen in subsequent experiments.

Emmanuel：明白了，谢谢你！

I see. Thank you.

吴军：Emmanuel，快点做完实验，晚饭后我们去打羽毛球，怎么样？

Emmanuel, hurry up and finish the experiment. We will play badminton after dinner. Can you play badminton?

Emmanuel：我刚好会打羽毛球，我的技术还不错呢。

I can play badminton rather well.

吴军：羽毛球是我们实验室的传统优势项目，曹教授就是羽毛球好手。在每年材料学院组织的"轻舞飞扬"师生羽毛球比赛中，我们实验室多次拿到了团体冠军。今晚，把咱们实验室外籍学生都叫上，选拔出水平最好的选手作为我们的外援。

Badminton is the traditional game of our laboratory, and Professor Cao is a good badminton player. In the "Dancing with Badminton" teacher-student badminton competition organized by the School of Materials and Science every year, our laboratory has won the team championship many times. Tonight, we will call all the foreign students in our laboratory and select the best players as our foreign aid.

Emmanuel：好的，我要争取上场比赛的机会。

Okay, I will work hard for the chance to play.

 重点词汇

Keywords & expressions

考勤制度	attendance checking system
值日表	duty schedule

· 167 ·

圆底烧瓶	round bottom flask
烧杯	beaker
毫升	milliliter，mL
离心机	centrifuge
离心管	centrifuge tube
转子	rotor
电子天平	electronic balance
超声波清洗机	ultrasonic cleaner
聚乙烯醇	polyvinyl alcohol，PVA
缩醛化	acetalization
水银温度计	mercury thermometer
三口烧瓶	three-necked flask
球形冷凝管	spherical condenser，allihn condenser
机械搅拌器	mechanical stirrer
油浴加热	oil bath heating
克	gram，g
去离子水	deionized water
甲醛	formaldehyde
盐酸	hydrochloric acid
醋酸乙烯酯	vinyl acetate
乳液	emulsion
聚合	polymerization
乳化剂	emulsifier
引发剂	initiator
单体聚合	monomer polymerization
过硫酸铵	ammonium persulfate
滴液漏斗	dropping funnel
回流冷凝管	reflux condenser

恒温浴槽	thermostatic bath
碳酸氢钠	sodium bicarbonate
邻苯二甲酸二丁酯	o-benzene dibutyl phthalate
乳胶	latex
培养皿	petri dish
烘箱	oven
氢氧化物	hydroxide
氧化亚铜	cuprous oxide
摩尔	mole
氯化铜	copper chloride
抗坏血酸	ascorbic acid
乙醇	ethanol
氯化镍	nickel chloride
氯化铁	ferric chloride
悬浊液	suspension
真空干燥	vacuum drying
刻蚀	etching
电催化性能	electrocatalytic properties

3.3 课题组的组会
Group Seminar

低维纳米材料合成方法

Emmanuel 在课题组的组会上向曹教授请教实验方案。

Emmanuel asks Prof. Cao about the experiment scheme in the group seminar.

Emmanuel：曹教授，您好。怎么才能化学合成出低维纳米材料呢？

Hello, Prof. Cao, how shall we chemically synthesize the low-dimensional nanomaterials?

曹：合成和工艺，这是材料科学四要素之一，需要根据你合成的目标产物去仔细选择合成技术和工艺方案。

Synthesis & Processing is one of the four basic elements of research at MSE. You need to carefully select the techniques and well-design the experimental route according to the target product you are synthesizing.

Emmanuel：您能介绍一下有哪些化学合成技术吗？

Could you introduce some chemical synthesis techniques?

曹：总的来说，实验室合成低维纳米材料分为基于液相-固相转变的技术和气相-固相转变的技术。

In general, laboratory synthesis techniques of low-dimensional nanomaterials can be classified as transition based on liquid-solid phase and transition based on vapor-solid phase.

Emmanuel：有哪些液相合成的技术呢？

What are the techniques for liquid phase synthesis?

曹：液相法有化学共沉淀法、溶胶-凝胶法、水热或者溶剂热合成法等。化学共沉淀法是将多种金属盐在溶液中共同发生化学反应，生成不溶性的沉淀物微粉。化学共沉淀法操作简单，需要对反应体系的酸碱度有精确的调控。溶胶-凝胶法是先将醇盐水解得到溶胶，再凝胶化，最后焙烧得到无机纳米材料。它可以很好控制不同组分的化学计量比，适合制备多组分纳米材料。水热法或者溶剂法需要在高压釜中进行。合成的关键参数是对温度和压强的控制。水热法通常合成氧化物纳米材料，溶剂热法用于合成碳化物、氮化物等纳米材料。

Liquid-phase synthesis techniques include chemical co-precipitation method, sol-gel method, hydrothermal or solvent thermal method, etc. Chemical co-precipitation produces insoluble precipitate nano-powders by the chemical reaction of one or more metal salts in solution. The chemical co-precipitation is easy to operate and needs precise control of the pH value of reaction system. The sol-gel method requires that we firstly form the sol by dissolving the alcohol brine, then gelatinize it, and finally obtain the inorganic nanomaterials by calcination. Sol-gel can control the stoichiometric ratio of different components well and is suitable for the preparation of multi-component nanomaterials. Hydrothermal method or solvent method needs to be carried out in an autoclave. The key parameter of synthesis is the control of temperature and pressure. Oxide nanomaterials are usually synthesized by hydrothermal method, and carbide or nitride nanomaterials are synthesized by solvent thermal method.

Emmanuel：有哪些气相合成技术呢？

What are the techniques for vapor phase synthesis?

曹：气相法包括化学气相沉积、溅射法、真空蒸发法等。气相法通过调节工艺既可以合成低维纳米材料，也可以在基底上沉积二维薄膜材料。气相合成法通常需要在反应前使用真空泵来制造一个清洁的真空背景。

Vapor-phase synthesis techniques include chemical vapor deposition (CVD), sputtering, vacuum evaporation, etc. The vapor-phase method can be used to synthesize low-dimensional nanomaterials or to deposit two-dimensional thin films on the substrate by adjusting the process. Vapor-phase synthesis usually requires the employ of a vacuum pump to create a clean vacuum background before the reaction.

Emmanuel：您能详细地讲讲这几种气相合成方法吗？

Could you please elaborate on these vapor-phase synthesis techniques?

曹：化学气相沉积是一种应用广泛的重要技术，它采用气相前驱体作为反应原料，在衬底表面发生化学反应，生成纳米材料或者薄膜材料，并且可以通过等离子体等辅助手段来降低反应温度。溅射法是利用等离子体中阳离子撞击固体靶材，通过动量传递的原理将靶材中的原子激发出来，在基底上形成薄膜。在光电解水研究中，我们要用溅射法沉积一层几百纳米厚的金属层作为析氢反应的背电极。真空蒸发法是一种原理简单的镀膜方法。在高真空环境下，采用高纯粉体作为原料，通常使用电子束加热，形成气相原子，在基底上沉积成薄膜。

Chemical vapor deposition (CVD) is an important technique that has been widely used. It uses gaseous precursor as the raw material in reactions to produce nano-materials or thin films by chemical reaction on the substrate surface. And the reaction temperature can be lowered by means of plasma and other auxiliary methods. Sputtering method uses cations in the plasma to collide with solid target material, and the atoms in the target material are excited by the principle of momentum transfer to deposit a thin film on the substrate. For example, in the photo-electrolysis water experiment, a metal film with several hundred nanometers thick is deposited by sputtering method as the back electrode of hydrogen evolution reaction. Vacuum evaporation is a simple filming method. In a high vacuum environment, high purity powder is used as raw material, usually heated by electron beam to form vapor-phase atoms, which are deposited on the substrate to form a thin film.

Emmanuel: 那么，具有特殊形貌的低维纳米材料是怎么合成的？

Then, how to synthesize the low-dimensional nanomaterials with some special morphology?

曹：在低维纳米材料合成过程中还有很多独特而有效的技巧。例如：有一种气液固生长机制，是在衬底上或者原料里掺杂添加微量的金属，高温下形成了金属液滴，能起到催化作用；气相反应原子不断在金属液滴中溶解，又从另一端不断析出，实现一维纳米形貌的生长。另外，在液相合成中添加表面活性剂会促进纳米晶粒的某一个晶面择优生长，从而获得特殊形貌的低维纳米材料。

There are also many unique and effective techniques in the synthesis of low-dimensional nano-materials. For instance, there is a vapor-liquid solid (VLS) growth mechanism, in which certain microcomponent metals is added or doped into the raw materials or on the substrate to form metal droplets at high temperature that can play a catalytic role. The precursor vapor atoms are continuously dissolved in the metal droplet and continuously precipitated from the other side to realize the growth of one-dimensional nano-meter morphology. In addition, the addition of some surfactant in the liquid phase synthesis can promote the selected preferred growth of a certain crystal surface of the generated nanograins so as to obtain the low-dimensional nano-materials with special morphology.

Emmanuel：谢谢曹教授的指导，我会努力去掌握纳米材料的合成技术。

Prof. Cao, thank you for your instruction. I will try my best to master the synthesis techniques of nano-materials.

曹：Emmanuel，那这两周你做了哪些实验？

Emmanuel, so, what experiments did you do in the last two weeks?

Emmanuel：曹老师，我什么也没有做呢。上次您不是告诉我，让我"不要着急，慢慢来"吗？

Prof. Cao, I have done nothing. I thought you told me last time, "don't worry, take it easy and slowly."

曹：这是你对中文语意理解上的偏差。"慢慢来"在中文语境中的含义，指的是你在工作初期可以进行一定的适应，不要在精神上负担过重。可是，你也要尽快调整自己，按照工作要求，提高工作效率，推进工作进度。而不是把时间都用来"摸鱼"，没有任何进展。

Well, it is a deviation in your understanding of Chinese linguistic nuance. The meaning of "take it easy and slowly" in Chinese context is that you can adapt in the early stages of the job without being overburdened in mind. However, you should adjust yourself as soon as you can, and improve working efficiency, push project progress according to the project requirements. Instead of laiding back and messing around all the time and get nothing.

Emmanuel：好的，老师。我知道了，我会努力的。

Yes, professor! I understand. I will try my best.

曹：其他学生开始顺序汇报上两周的实验数据、

实验结果和下两周的实验计划。

Now, the rest of students take turns to report your last two-week's experimental data, experimental results and the next two-week's experiment plan.

重点词汇
Keywords & expressions

液相－固相转变	liquid-solid phase transition
液相法	liquid-phase synthesis
化学共沉淀法	chemical co-precipitation method
溶胶－凝胶法	sol-gel method
凝胶	gel
化学计量比	stoichiometric ratio
高压釜	autoclave
水热合成	hydrothermal synthesis
溶剂热	solvent thermal
化学气相沉积	chemical vapor deposition, CVD
溅射法	sputtering
真空蒸发法	vacuum evaporation
真空泵	vacuum pump
气相前驱体	precursor
等离子体	plasma
靶材	target
形貌	morphology
表面活性剂	surface active agent
择优生长	preferred growth

3.4 材料样品的表征与测试
Characterization and Testing of Material Samples

材料样品的表征与测试

Emmanuel 在实验室里做了一段时间纳米材料的合成实验，获得了一批实验样品。Emmanuel 向同一实验室的刘钰、王国庆、吴军请教。

Emmanuel has done the nanomaterials synthesis experiments for a period of time in the laboratory, and produced a batch of experimental samples. Then, he asks peer students in the same lab, Liu Yu, Wang Guoqing and Wu Jun, for advice.

Emmanuel：“老铁”们，我做了很长时间实验，也得到很多样品了。下面该做什么？

Hi, buddies! I've been doing experiments for a long time and I've got a lot of samples. What should I do next?

刘：我们看看材料科学的四要素。下一步就是表征"组成和结构"，测试"材料性能"，找出材料性能与其成分及显微结构之间的内在关系。

Well, let us have a look at the four basic elements of research at MSE. What you should do next is to characterize the composition & structure, and testing properties of materials, and find the internal relationship between microstructure and their properties.

Emmanuel：怎么表征样品的"组成和结构"？

How to characterize the "composition & structure" of materials samples?

王："组成和结构"的表征方法最基本的有两种,即用于材料物相分析的X射线衍射分析和直接观察材料形貌的电镜分析。X射线衍射分析术可以表征晶体材料的点阵类型和晶粒大小,并且有完整详备的材料结构衍射谱数据库,可以对照检索材料的晶体结构,功能非常强大。扫描电子显微术和透射电子显微术可以将显微组织的观察尺度推进到纳米层次。大部分的电子显微镜都附加了能谱仪,具有元素种类和含量的分析功能,高分辨扫描电镜还可以清楚显示材料的晶格条纹图像。这对于低维纳米材料来说,是必不可缺的表征手段。

There are two basic characterization methods for "composition & structure." That is, the X-ray Diffraction (XRD) for material phase analysis and the electron microscopy for morphology observation directly. XRD can characterize the crystal lattice type and the grain size of materials sample. There is a complete and detailed database of diffraction spectrum of material structure that can be indexed by comparison, which has a very powerful function. Scanning electron microscopy (SEM) and transmission electron microscopy (TEM) are the most commonly used electron microscopy techniques, which can promote the observation scale of microstructure to nanoscale. Most of SEM and TEM have equipped energy dispersive spectrometer(EDS) which possesses the function of element type and content analysis, and the high resolution scanning electron microscopy(HRTEM) can also clearly show the lattice fringe pattern of crystal samples. It is an essential characterization method for low-dimensional nanomaterials.

Emmanuel：还有哪些材料的表征技术？

In addition, are there any other characterization techniques of materials?

吴：对于有机高分子材料来说，紫外光谱、红外光谱、质谱和核磁共振谱，这四大光谱是最核心的表征方式，可以分析出复杂高聚物材料中不同的官能团、价键和能带宽度。X射线光电子能谱是对所有材料通用的表征手段，可以检测出材料很薄表面层上的元素含量和元素价态。

For organic polymer materials, ultraviolet-visible spectroscopy(UV), infrared spectroscopy(IR), mass spectrum(MS) and nuclear magnetic resonance spectroscopy(NMR) are the four core characterization methods, which can analyze the different functional groups, the structure valence bond and the band width in complex polymer materials. X-ray photoelectron spectroscopy(XPS) is also a universal characterization method for all materials. It can detect the trace content and valence state of elements in a very thin surface depth.

Emmanuel：去哪儿做这些分析测试？

But, where shall I do these characterization analysis of samples?

王： 在咱们五号楼的十层有一个全新建成的先进材料实验中心，那儿就可以测试表征了。这是北京理工大学依托材料学院建设的公共实验平台，拥有各种类型的测试分析设备，总价值超过8 000万人民币，实验平台面积有1 300平米。敞亮，大气，有着"现代化、集约式、开放型"的新理念。

On the tenth floor of our No. 5 building, there is a newly built Experiment Center of Advanced Materials, where the characterization analysis of samples can be carried out. It is the first public experiment platform constructed and run by BIT based at the School of MSE, which owns various kinds of characterization analysis equipment valued over 80 million RMB in total, and covers an area of 1,300 square meters. The Center is bright and grand, representing the new concept of a "modern, intensive and open" platform.

吴： 实验中心建成以前，需要测试表征的时候，我们只能往校外机构送样品和等待结果，花费很多宝贵的时间。自从中心建成后，制备出的新材料样品可以马上送到10层，很快就能在中心的平台上进行测试，大大缩短了实验周期，提高了科研效率。

Before the establishment of the experimental center, I had to send samples to the off-campus agencies and wait for the results when I needed to do some testing and characterization analysis for my samples, which was time consuming. Now I can send the newly as-synthesized samples to the 10th floor immediately, and the samples will be tested soon on the characterization platform of the experimental center, which greatly shortens the experimental period and improves the efficiency of scientific research.

Emmanuel: 太好了，拥有自己的测试实验平台真便利呀！

Very nice! It is so convenient to own characterization and testing platform ourselves!

先进材料实验中心
Experimental Center of Advanced Materials

刘: 先别高兴，我还要考考你，材料显微结构和晶体结构测试表征的原理是什么？不能知其然而不知其所以然。

Don't get so excited yet. I will give you a test first. What are the principles of microstructure and crystal structure characterization of materials? You should not only know what it is, but also know why it is the way now.

Emmanuel： 这个问题和这句话的中文对我来说都太难了，我真不知道怎么回答。

The question and the Chinese that you said are so difficult that I really don't know how to answer.

刘： 利用不同频段的电磁波辐射、不同能量的电子、离子、中子与被测试材料相互作用，分析作用后粒子的携带信息就可以表征出材料的组织形态、结构与化学成分。这就是分析表征技术的物理学基础。

The crystal structure, morphology and chemical composition of samples can be characterized with the interaction of electromagnetic radiation at different frequency, electrons, ions and neutrons carrying different energy, react with the tested materials samples. This is the physical basis of analytical characterization techniques.

Emmanuel： 谢谢刘同学。另外一个问题，合成样品的物理化学性质去哪儿测试呀？

Thank you, Liu Yu. Another question is: Where can we test the properties of as-synthesized samples?

王： 我们实验室自己就可以测试，实验室有电化学工作站、原位半导体性能综合测试仪、振动样品磁强计等设备，可以测试材料的电学、

第三章 学有所成 不负韶华

光学、磁学和半导体性质。

You can test it in our laboratory. There are electrochemical workstation, *in situ* semiconductor performance comprehensive tester, vibration sample magnetometer and other testing equipment, which can test the electrical, optical, magnetic and semiconductor properties of materials.

Emmanuel：谢谢"老铁"们！我找到前进的道路了！

Thank you, buddies. I've found my way forward!

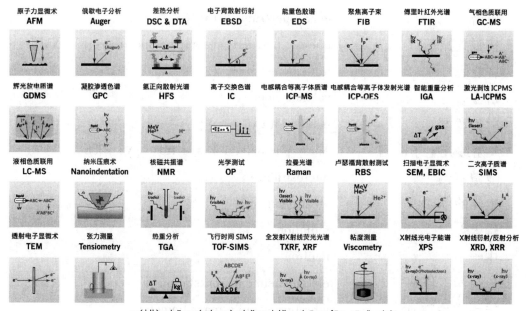

材料科学的各种表征分析技术

Various Characterization and Analysis Techniques for Materials Science

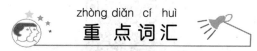

Keywords & expressions

表征	characterization

中文	English
X射线衍射	X-ray diffraction，XRD
光谱	spectrum
扫描电子显微术	scanning electron microscopy，SEM
透射电子显微术	transmission electron microscopy，TEM
能谱仪	energy dispersive spectrometer，EDS
高分辨	high-resolution
晶格条纹	lattice fringe
紫外光谱	ultraviolet-visible spectroscopy，UV
红外光谱	infrared spectroscopy，IR
质谱	mass spectrum，MS
核磁共振谱	nuclear magnetic resonance spectroscopy，NMR
官能团	functional group
价键	valence bond
能带宽度	band width
X射线光电子能谱	X-ray photoelectron spectroscopy，XPS
显微结构	microstructure
电磁的	electromagnetic
辐射	radiation
中子	neutron
电化学工作站	electrochemical workstation
振动样品磁强计	vibration sample magnetometer

3.5 撰写科学论文
Writing a Scientific Manuscript

撰写科学论文

一次例行组会结束后，曹教授让Emmanuel去他的办公室。

Prof. Cao asks Emmanuel to go to his office after one regular seminar.

曹教授：Emmanuel，经过你的多次实验，已经得到了一些好的实验结果，应该把数据及时地分析和总结，写出科学论文了。

Emmanuel, you have obtained some positive results after trials and errors. Now, you should compile and analyze the results to write a scientific manuscript for publication in an academic journal.

Emmanuel：为什么要写科学论文？

Why should I write a scientific manuscript?

曹："不成文，便成仁"，不发表，就灭亡，这就是学术生涯的写照。论文的数量和质量是你科研事业的敲门砖。

"Publish or perish" reflects the reality of academic life. Both quantity and quality of published papers are essential for advancing the career of a Ph. D. candidate.

Emmanuel：怎么撰写一篇科学论文？

How to write a scientific manuscript?

曹：典型的科学论文通常包括：标题、作者和科研单位、摘要、关键词、论文主体部分、致谢和参考文献。主体部分又包括引言、研究方法和实验步骤、实验结果和讨论、结论，是论文的核心内容。因为科学论文不是文学性的散文，这样的文章结构可以使读者快速找到他们感兴趣的信息和数据。把信息放错地方会使读者感到迷惑。

A typical science paper includes a title, authors and their affiliations, abstract, key words, main body (introduction, experimental methods and procedures, results and discussion, conclusion or summary), acknowledgements and references. Since scientific manuscripts are not equivalent to essays, these sections are designed to help readers to locate the information of their interest quickly. Placing information in the wrong section will confuse readers.

Emmanuel：撰写科学论文好难呀。

Writing a scientific manuscript is so hard!

曹：难是肯定的。没有人能够第一次就写好科学论文。写完一遍以后，要反复进行修改。要尽你最大努力去写作。同时，即便文章发表了，却没人看，那也等于没有发表。

No one could write a perfect scientific manuscript for the first try. You should revise it again and again. Your paper is worthless if no one reads it even if it has been published.

Emmanuel：我们为什么需要在写作上这么认真努力？

Why is there a need to make such a significant effort to write it?

曹：论文的读者可能是刚进入这个领域的新手：大学

生和研究生,也会有对这个领域知识有不同程度了解的专家,包括潜在的审稿人。只有可以被充分理解的研究结果才会被其他研究人员跟进和引用,而论文被他人引用的次数常常用来衡量研究的影响力。

The potential readers of your paper have a diverse level of expertise in research field. They may be beginners, such as undergraduate students and graduates, or well-established experts (potential peer reviewers). Only a well explained paper enables others to follow the lead and citation. The number of citations by others is a measure of the impact of a research.

Emmanuel：论文撰写完成以后,怎么投寄到学术期刊上?要投寄到什么样的期刊呢?

When I finish my manuscript, what kind of journal should I submit it to?

曹：各个学术期刊对稿件的要求是不一样的,在期刊的"作者须知"会有具体的解说,你需要仔细阅读和了解。投寄科学论文时,通常还要附上投稿信。投稿信里要简叙所投论文的主要发现、创新点和重要意义,以及声明论文符合对稿件评阅的利益冲突、竞争性要求和科学伦理要求等。由于对论文的篇幅有限制,还需要附上补充的证据材料。

尽管将论文发表在顶尖的学术期刊上会引发更多的关注,但是,当我们将期刊的重要性置于科学发现本身之上时,等于将自己在学术界置于平俗之辈。

Different academic journals have different requirements for manuscripts. You should read the guide for authors carefully to fully understand their requirements. When you submit a scientific manuscript, you need to attach a cover letter. A cover letter should briefly describe the main findings and significance of the submitted paper, the name of the proposed journal, the conflicts of interest and competitive requirements for the review of the paper, and the declaration that the paper meets the requirements of scientific ethics. Some academic journals also require that supplementary materials be attached due to the limitation on the length of manuscripts.

Although there are good reasons for publishing papers on top journals where they are more likely to be read, when we put more attention on the journal rather than the science itself, we tend to lose our virtue of striving for being a top scientist.

Emmanuel: 这样论文就可以发表了吗?

Then, can the manuscript be published?

曹: 论文寄给杂志编辑后,首先要经过重复率检查。重复率超过15%的论文,是会被直接拒稿的。照抄别人文章中的句子在科学上是不道德的,这表明了作者不愿思考,只会走捷径,不具备真正科研工作者的素质。一定要使用别人的原句时，必须加上引号，引索到原始文献。论文里的原创性结果得到编辑认可后，他才会将论文交给同行专家来评议。通常会有3-4名同行专家来审阅你的论文。编辑汇总了专家的意见会对论文给出结果：接受、小修改、大修改或者拒稿。人世间最痛苦的事莫过于收到编辑来信，第一句话就是：我们遗憾地通知您……

Not exactly. After a manuscript is submitted to a journal editor, it should first go through duplicate checking. A paper with the repeat rate of more than 15% will be rejected outright. It is unethical to copy others' sentences, which shows that the author does not want to think, only takes shortcuts, and therefore, does not possess the quality of a real scientific researcher. If it is absolutely necessary to use the sentence from other papers, add quotation marks and cite original reference.

Only after the original results in the manuscript have been approved by the editor, he or she will hand it over to peers for review. Your manuscript is usually reviewed by two or three peer experts. The editor collects the opinions of the experts and gives the results of the paper: accepting it, minor revision, major revision or rejection. The saddest thing in the world is receiving a letter from the editor beginning with "We are sorry to inform you"...

Emmanuel：曹教授，怎么才能规避学术期刊编辑的大斧呢？
Prof. Cao, how to avoid the editor's scythe?

曹：首先是论文有创新性的研究结果。其次，还是回到论文写作。好的科学论文要主动迎合读者和评审人的预期。也就是说，文章的逻辑要清晰，要让读者不费力理解你的论文，不要试图展示从帽子里变出小兔子的把戏。第三点，在论文投寄以前，需要自己用挑剔的眼光去看待论文，预先回答审稿人的所有可能的问题。

First and foremost, the manuscript must possess original and innovative research results. Second, let's go back to manuscript writing itself. Recipe for a quality scientific paper: fulfill the reader's and reviewer's expectations. That is, keep the logic clear and make it easy for the reader to understand. Don't play tricks like pulling out bunnies out of the hat. Third, you need to look at your manuscript critically and answer all of the reviewer's possible questions in advance before you submit it.

Emmanuel：我有点懂了。

I understand a little bit.

曹：写论文的过程，是你深入思考研究方法成功与失败，寻求实验结果的解释及隐含意义，以及与相关研究进行比较的过程。因此也是科学研究不可分割的一个重要环节。

The process of writing a research paper is one in which you rationalize the success and failure of the research method employed, search for the implications and other possible interpretations of the results obtained, and compare or contrast your work with other related studies. Therefore, it is an integral part of scientific research.

Emmanuel：谢谢曹教授，我会努力去写好我的科学论文。

Thank you, Prof. Cao. I will try my best to write my scientific paper well.

重点词汇
Keywords & expressions

科学论文	scientific manuscript
摘要	abstract
关键词	keywords
致谢	acknowledgements
参考文献	references
同行审稿	peer review
引用	citation
投稿信	cover letter
补充材料	supplementary materials
重复率	repeat rate
拒稿	rejection

3.6 准备学位答辩的流程
Procedures for the Defense of the Academic Degree

如何准备博士学位答辩

经过四年的实验室工作，Emmanuel 准备进入毕业流程。他向马老师咨询毕业答辩前的准备工作。

After four years of laboratory work, Emmanuel is ready to enter the graduation process. He consults Ms. Ma about preparations before graduation defense.

Emmanuel: 马老师,您好。我想申请毕业答辩,但是不知道需要做什么准备工作,你能够帮我吗?

Hello, Mr. Ma. I want to apply for graduation defense, but don't know what preparations are needed. Can you help me?

马: 当然可以。首先,你必须确认你已经满足学校对于博士毕业的要求。

Of course. First of all, you must confirm that you have met the school's requirements for doctoral graduation.

Emmanuel: 北京理工大学对博士毕业有哪些具体要求?

What are the specific requirements for doctoral graduation in Beijing Institute of Technology?

马: 已经发表的学术文章的质量和数量达到学校学术委员会的学位评定要求并且完成博士学位论文,你就可以开始提交你的学位申请了。

You have to confirm that the quality and quantity of the academic articles you have published meet the degree evaluation requirements of the university academic committee, and after completing your dissertation, you can begin to submit your degree application.

Emmanuel: 学校对文章的具体要求是什么呢?

What are the specific requirements of the school for articles?

马: 发表的文章必须以你为第一作者,导师作为通

第三章　学有所成　不负韶华

讯作者，论文的第一署名单位必须是北京理工大学，以表明这是你在读博士期间的科研成果。此外，已经公开发表论文要提供期刊的名称卷期号和页码已录用；还未发表的论文，需要提供DOI号。

The article you have published must regard you as the first author, your supervisor as the corresponding author, and the first signature of the paper must be Beijing Institute of Technology, to show that this is your research achievement during your Ph. D. In addition, the name of the journal, volume number and page number should be provided for published papers. For accepted unpublished papers, DOI numbers are required.

Emmanuel: 我的科研成果已经满足学校学位评定的要求，我也写完了我的博士论文，曹教授正在审阅并给我修改指导。

My scientific research results have met the requirements of the school degree evaluation, and I have finished my doctoral dissertation. Professor Cao is reviewing it and giving me revision guidance.

马: 好的。你可以用你的学号和密码登录到研究生管理系统。在这个管理系统中，进入到学位授予工作环节。你必须按照系统提示一步一步去填写所有信息，完成审查工作。这些环节每一步都要认真去完成。当前环节完成

· 193 ·

后，指示条会由红变绿，然后你才可以进行下一环节的填报申请。

OK. You can log in to the graduate management system with your student ID and password. In this management system, when you enter the degree granting process, you can follow the system prompts to fill in all the information step by step and complete the review work. Each step of these links must be carefully completed. After the current link is completed, the indicator bar will turn from red to green, and you can proceed to the next link to fill in the application.

Emmanuel：下一个步骤是什么？

What is the next step?

马：你在系统里上传你最终博士论文的电子版以后，还要申请进行查重检测。当你的论文重复率低于学校的要求，才算通过。

After you upload the electronic version of your final doctoral dissertation in the system, you have to apply for duplicate checking. Your paper will be considered passed when the probability of repetition is lower than that of the school's requirement.

Emmanuel：知道了。还有吗？

Understood. Is there any more information I need to know about?

马：你要告诉导师你已经完成了学位论文的网上提交，导师会在他的管理系统中，对你的学位论文填写评语，进行评价。当导师完成了审核后，你才能进入论文的评阅阶段。

第三章 学有所成不负韶华

You have to tell your supervisor that you have completed the online submission of your dissertation, and your supervisor will fill in comments and evaluate your dissertation in his management system. You can enter the review stage of the paper after the supervisor completes the review.

Emmanuel：论文评阅阶段具体是怎样进行的？

How does the paper review stage go?

马：在论文评阅阶段，必须有五位博士生导师对你的论文进行评价，一般是三位导师盲审和两位导师明审。当五位导师对你的论文评价都是A且一致同意答辩，你才能够参加答辩。如果有评阅老师认为你的学位论文评分仅为B、C甚至D，那么你需要对论文进行修改，甚至延期毕业。

During the paper review stage, there must be five doctoral supervisors to evaluate your paper, of whom, generally, three anonymous supervisors will review it and two supervisors openly review it. When five supervisors evaluate your paper as A and all agree to defend your paper, you can participate in the subsequent defense. If a reviewing teacher thinks your dissertation is graded B, C or even D, then you need to revise your paper or even postpone graduation.

Emmanuel：之后我就可以进行博士毕业答辩了吗？

Can I proceed to the Ph. D. graduation defense afterwards?

马：差不多。当论文评阅结束后，就正式进入了答辩阶段。我和你的导师曹教授商量邀请至少五位成员组成答辩委员会。要确保答辩委员都是高级职称，并且具有博导资质，通常由我来担任答辩秘书。

Almost. After the paper review, it will officially enter the defense stage. I will discuss with your advisor, Professor Cao, about inviting at least five members to form a defense committee. It is necessary to ensure that all of the defense members have senior titles and have Ph. D. supervisor qualifications. I usually serve as a defense secretary.

Emmanuel：毕业答辩之前还有这么多工作需要做啊！

There is still so much work to do before graduation defense!

马：当然。博士学位答辩是一件非常严肃和隆重的学术活动，任何环节都不能出现瑕疵。答辩前，你要事先给每一位答辩委员准备好由研究生院学位评定委员会盖章的答辩表决票和评分表。答辩时，你的论文报告时间大约是限定在30分钟以内，然后由答辩委员们针对你的论文有15分钟的自由提问。最后，答辩委员对你的博士论文答辩进行表决和打分。表决结果可以是同意、不同意或者弃权。

Of course. The Ph. D. defense is a very serious and solemn academic activity, and there must be no defects at any stage. Before the defense, you must prepare the defense ballots stamped by the Graduate School Degree Evaluation Committee for each respondent in advance. During the defense, the oral presentation time is about 30 minutes, and then the defense committee members are free to ask questions about your dissertation for 15 minutes. Finally, the defense committee members will vote on your doctoral dissertation defense. The voting result would be pass, fail, or abstention.

Emmanuel：万一有不同意的投票岂不是太恐怖了？
Wouldn't it be too horrible if someone vote fail?

马：所以在正式答辩以前，我们要组织一次预答辩，帮你进行改进和提高。
So before the formal defense, we will organize a pre-defense to help you improve your defense performance.

Emmanuel：我已经开始紧张了……
I'm already nervous.

马："奥利给"，加油！
Come on, you can do it!

Emmanuel：哈哈。谢谢马老师！
Thank you, Ms. Ma!

经过一个半月的精心准备，Emmanuel 顺利通过了博士论文答辩，被授予工学博士学位。他终于可以奔向前景光明的职业生涯。

After one and a half months of careful preparation, Emmanuel successfully passed the defense of his doctoral dissertation and was awarded the doctorate degree of Engineering. Now, he is heading for a bright and promising career at last.

wǒ men bì yè le
我 们 毕 业 了
We Have Graduated

 zhòng diǎn cí huì
重 点 词 汇

Keywords & expressions

毕业答辩	graduation defense
学术委员会	academic committee
通讯作者	corresponding author
博士论文	doctoral dissertation
学号	student ID
研究生管理系统	postgraduate management system
查重	duplicate checking
盲审	blind review
明审	open review

第三章 学有所成 不负韶华

延期毕业	postpone graduation
答辩表决票	defense ballot
投票	vote
弃权	abstention
预答辩	pre-defense

永远的北理人
Forever BITers

跋

　　从改革开放打开国门伊始，到"一带一路"建设，我国拓展了国际交流新局面。这四十多年的历程一直贯穿着中华民族走向世界，在全球范围和各国的科学、技术、人文进行深度交汇。同时，日新月异、锐意创新的开放中国和底蕴厚重、韵味无穷的中华文化也吸引了越来越多的外籍人士来到中国，了解中国，在中国学习，以至定居中国。当科技的高速发展把人类社会缩小成一个地球村，我们选择了包容的心态，就可以拥抱整个世界；而你漠视拒绝它，就会回到孤立封闭的角落里。

　　随着中国国力的日益增强，提升在全球范围内文化、科技、价值理念层面上的辐射力，需要荟萃吸纳来自世界范围各种类型的有才能、有见识、高智商的专业人才，培养亲近和爱好中华文化的外籍人士，以汉唐胸襟构建人类命运共同体，对汉语交流就有了更高层次的要求。这就需要进一步在专业技术领域、在职场工作中、在科学研究中，使用汉语普通话进行深入的信息沟通、分享经验、交流观点、争论问题等等。如果在中国国内长期学习、生活、工作，还需借助英语或者其它语言作为第三方沟通工具，于情于理都不合时宜，效率也较为低下。汉语本身是很有魅力的表意语言文字，学习者只要努力去掌握一些高频词汇、常见表达和专业技术术语，就可以用汉语和中国研究人员实现快捷交流。

　　材料、信息、能源被誉为当代文明的三大支柱，材料科学也是新世纪六大高技术群体之一，无论是科学研究还是产业化应用，都有着宽广的前景。本书不是一本系统讲授材料科学全貌的中英文对照教材，也不是北京理工大学材料科学研究成果的宣传汇编。本书只是借助了材料科学基础知识和前沿研究的概念、术语、语言体系的表观形式，所要体现的是专业科技汉语交流本质，同时，它又确实地搭起了一座通往材料科学高级学位的桥梁。

作为本书背景的北京理工大学是一所国家历批次重点建设的研究型理工科大学。在加速高校国际化和世界一流大学建设的进程中，材料学院自2007年开始招收外籍研究生，迄今50多名外籍学生已经毕业，三分之二的留学生获得了博士学位，其他获得硕士学位。现在材料学院每年新进招收几十名外籍研究生，在读在研的外籍留学生有100余名。

2022年是北京理工大学材料学院建院20周年，祝愿材料学院在国际化建设的道路上快步前行、花果飘香、无远弗届！